The Reluctant Detective Goes North

A Martin Hayden Mystery

by
Adrian Spalding

Contents

- Chapter 1 1
- Chapter 2 12
- Chapter 3 24
- Chapter 4 39
- Chapter 5 51
- Chapter 6 67
- Chapter 7 83
- Chapter 8 91
- Chapter 9 103
- Chapter 10 119
- Chapter 11 127
- Chapter 12 134
- Chapter 13 152
- Chapter 14 160
- Chapter 15 172
- Chapter 16 182
- Chapter 17 186
- Chapter 18 203
- Chapter 19 223
- Chapter 20 235
- Chapter 21 246
- Chapter 22 261
- Chapter 23 268
- Author Notes 277
- A special thanks 278

The Reluctant Detective Goes North
Copyright © 2023 by Adrian Spalding.

All rights reserved. No part of this book may be reproduced in any form or by any electronic or mechanical means, including information storage and retrieval systems, without permission in writing from the author. The only exception is by a reviewer, who may quote short excerpts in a review.

This book is a work of fiction. Names, characters, places, and incidents either are products of the author's imagination or are used fictitiously. Any resemblance to actual persons, living or dead, events, or locales is entirely coincidental.

In memory of my nephew

Stephen Shanks

12th April 1978 – 23rd April 2023.

Chapter 1

"It was pretty scary, I can tell you," a wide-eyed Susan declared as she frantically secured her seat belt into place. Martin looked quizzically at her.

"Now, are you sure you have everything?"

"Yes of course. Anyway, as I was saying, it was scary."

"You have already told me that." Turning his attention back to driving, he started the engine of his beloved Honda Civic, then meticulously secured and adjusted his own seat belt.

"It was just too dark to see anything. All I could feel was the rough wood of a door in front of me which was unlocked. It should have been locked, that I knew, but it wasn't. As I pushed it, there was this weird glow coming from inside the shed. Well, when I say glow, it was more like an aurora, which as I opened the door further seemed to be getting brighter and brighter.

"I slipped into the shed. A really dirty, cluttered garden shed. The light was coming from a large flowerpot under the workbench. I was eye-level with it. I wanted to run, but I knew my legs were weak and would not support me. I couldn't walk, I had to crawl and I was somehow being drawn towards this flowerpot with the eerie green glow coming from it. I was terrified, honest."

"Yes, terrified, you've already told me," Martin sounded uninterested as he joined the slow-moving traffic once again, leaving the motorway services behind.

"Then the whole shed started to rattle and vibrate. The garden tools started to fall off their hooks landing really close to me. I thought I was going to get a rusty spade hitting my head. I was a sitting target."

"Crawling target," Martin corrected sarcastically.

"I was a target," Susan retorted sharply. "Then I got to the flowerpot, a big cat jumped out, jet black he was, with long claws drawn and ready to dig into my face. Totally scared, I just froze on the cold floor, then I woke up in a sweat. But it was oh so scary!"

"Really, who'd have thought it? It was a dream Susan, dreams are just figments of, in your case, a very warped, wild imagination."

"And I suppose all your dreams are sensible and well-ordered."

"Well, everyone tells me that I must dream, but I have yet to remember one. The minute I open my eyes whatever I was doing nocturnally in my subconscious just disappears from my memory. It makes for a fresh start to the day."

Martin was not exactly being honest in his statement that he never recalled his dreams. He did on occasions wake up after a night of mysterious activities, most of which made little sense. It was just that if he began to tell Susan about some of those he recalled, she would spend the rest of the journey to Grantham looking for a deep hidden meaning in a dream which he considered to be no more than the ramblings of a slumbering mind. All he wanted was to focus on the journey and get to Howard's wedding weekend on time.

It was a while since Martin had received the wedding invitation from one of the rugby players at the club where he watched and drank. The groom, Howard Phillips was at long last marrying Hanna, with whom he had been co-habiting for the last seven years. At the time Martin received the invite, which was for him and a guest, he had been dating a married woman who had since ended the affair, thus leaving Martin without a partner to take.

Not that Martin was one for keeping up appearances, yet he had no intention to turn up at the wedding alone, looking like 'Billy No Mates'. But currently he did not have a girlfriend, steady or casual. Another option would be to bring one of his drinking companions along. That would go against the unwritten social rules he and his friends followed. The rule stated clearly that when given an invitation to a wedding which extends to a guest of your choice, then that guest should be the opposite sex, hence a couple, reflecting the composition of the wedding couple. Since that unwritten rule was written, things had changed with the advent of same-sex couples. Hence the unwritten amendment read, bring a guest that you are in a relationship with.

Strictly speaking Susan and Martin were not in a sexual relationship, but for the purpose of the wedding invitation decree, Martin could describe them as in a relationship, albeit a business one. His social conscience was therefore clear, which was more than could be said for the northbound motorway, as the traffic slowly inched along ahead of him.

"Where's my scarf?" Susan piped up.

"The one you left on the table beside your coffee cup back at the service station?"

"Yes, oh I left it behind. I don't suppose…"

"No, I am not going back for a scarf that is now in the boot of this car." Martin smiled towards Susan who playfully punched him on the shoulder.

"This is exciting you know," Susan gleefully pointed out. "I haven't been to a wedding in years, the last time, I think, was a girl I went to Slimming World with. We got on like a house on fire, both of us didn't need to lose any weight really, it was just fun to make the others feel bad. She married a telephone engineer, didn't last long."

"Was he already engaged?" Martin commented.

"Very droll. Martin, you might be a lot of things, however a stand-up comic is not one of them. No, he wanted to move up to Liverpool for his job. She wouldn't move more than three miles from her mother. Irreconcilable differences, I think the term is. Good wedding though. I bet your stag night with a load of rugby players will be good. How many pubs do you intend on hitting?"

"The raucous night was a while back, I missed out on that one. Tonight will be a very dignified affair at some local restaurant, mainly because the groom's father will be there and he is, so I am told, a notable local citizen with a reputation to uphold. Sadly, no strippers or drinking games. I'm just sorry I must leave you on your own for the first evening. Will you be alright?"

"I'll be fine. I plan to soak in the bath and follow up with a movie on TV. Lots of 'me time'. Which reminds me, your stars for the weekend. Where are we?" Susan opened her phone, scrolling down until she came to Martin's star sign of Pisces.

"This is you, Pisces, *'a great time for you to think about going away.'* Well, that's spot on. *'You are adaptable enough to have fun with whatever comes your way. Invite people to go with you who share similar interests, so you won't have to argue about every little decision.'* As if we would. *'The point of a vacation is to have fun.'* I'd say we're in for a good weekend. Just one last word of warning here, *'A saucy name could thwart your enjoyment.'* Oh dear, that's a bit of a bummer. Saucy names, hmm, I suppose we'll have to avoid people like Dick or Willy. I'm guessing none of your posh friends have such common names."

"I'm sure there are at least a few Richards and Williams in my social circle. More of a worry though, if I am going to believe that the horoscope tripe you read out is correct, is that the groom is called Howard Phillips."

"Well, that's not rude, is it?"

"No, but his initials are saucy, H.P."

"What? Ah the brown sauce, best watch out for him then."

***

Originally Martin was going to invite Jenny, his lover, to the wedding, until she decided her husband did love her after all and ended what had been a torrid affair with him. When Susan had heard of it, she felt sympathy for Martin, because as nice as he was, he did not seem to be lucky with girlfriends. Or at least the ones that she knew about as he was not one to share all his experiences with her.

Maybe, she thought, he was a little too nice, and only wanted to have fun and not get too serious in a relationship. Susan knew she was not an expert in that department, far from it. Her only skill was to choose the wrong type of man. None of her boyfriends had been either faithful or loving, and in Bradley's case, he also had a bad sense of timing.

She recalled the evening that Martin had taken her to a posh restaurant to prove that he was happy to be with her socially, disproving her belief that she was too common for him. He even took her home. Awkwardly they had stood outside of her flat, Susan was on the verge of inviting him in for a night cap. It was Bradley, her then semi-boyfriend, arriving on the scene that broke the moment. Well, Susan felt it was a moment and she hoped Martin had felt the same way.

"When are you going to get married?" Susan asked bluntly, something she was proficient at.

"You are sounding more like my mother every day."

"That's not an answer to my question. I know you're an old romantic at heart. You were engaged to Paula years ago, planning to marry her in defiance of your family. That's the sort of thing Mills and Boon stories are made of."

"And just like any romantic fiction, the woman swindled me out of thousands of pounds and proved my family right. Is that how all Mills and Boons end up?"

Knowing Paula had been a difficult time for Martin. Back then he believed in true love, fate bringing together two people from different backgrounds, their love able to overcome any barrier. Maybe back then he did subscribe to the romance of endearing love stories, but she did betray him. All during their engagement, she was scheming to defraud him out of as much money as she could.

She was the reason that Martin turned to simple affairs with married women. It was less complex and no long-term commitment was involved. That is until Jenny arrived, and Martin once again imagined a prolonged relationship, one where Jenny did indeed leave her husband and set up home with him. But then she decided that she loved her husband and dropped Martin like a stone. Maybe he was not marriage material after all, either that or he had made some poor decisions in the romance department.

Yet his mother's recent illness had made him focus on the reality that one day she would die, and he would be alone in the world. A middle-aged Martin, living off ready meals and watching TV soaps was something he planned to avoid at any cost.

At least he had a colleague and good friend in Susan. It felt good to have her by his side and her presence allowed him to turn up at the wedding with a guest. He was now looking forward to the weekend, although if he had had a crystal ball handy to foresee the future, he might have just declined the invitation in the first place.

***

They arrived at Harby Hall Hotel a little later than Martin had planned, yet still in plenty of time before the planned quick drink with the groom and his best man so he could introduce Susan to them. The Harby Hall Hotel, just outside Grantham, built more than a century ago, still retained some of the original features. The reception was not one of those elements, it was contemporary and streamlined. Martin and Susan set their suitcases down in front of the light oak desk and spoke to the tall receptionist who stood behind a computer screen.

"We are with the Phillips's wedding party. The groom has booked on my behalf, Martin Hayden."

The receptionist consulted her computer screen. All were standing in anticipation before she inquired, "Mrs Hayden?" looking at Susan.

"Oh no, I'm Susan, Susan Morris."

The receptionist looked confused before once again checking her screen. She was clearly in no great rush. As she bent forward, a whisp of her jet-black hair flopped in front of her eyes, she flicked it back with her hand. Then her head began nodding negatively, she was working herself up to a loud tut of frustration. She had thirty more minutes of her shift to work and now she gets the troublemakers.

"I think I can explain," Martin sounded almost apologetic. "I spoke to Howard, the groom, Susan and I are just friends, so it is not appropriate for us to share a room together. He called me yesterday and said you had some spare rooms. If I can book an extra room, I'll pay for that one as well."

"But," the receptionist rudely pointed out, "Mr Phillips has already booked a double room for you and a guest." Her eyes cast a disapproving look at Susan. "He booked four rooms for his guests who were not part of the family bridal group. You are the last couple to arrive."

"Yes," Martin said, "but as mentioned we are not a couple. A double room is not the preferred option. Can I book another room enabling us to sleep in different rooms?"

"He snores terribly," Susan joked. The look on Martin's face told her he did not find it amusing nor apparently did the hotel employee.

"We don't have any spare rooms; we are fully booked."

"Are you sure? Howard told me only yesterday that you had three spare rooms. I'd like one of those, please."

"Well, if you'd asked me yesterday, I would have let you have one of those spare rooms, as they were spare yesterday when I spoke to Mr Phillips Junior. Today they're booked, we had a reservation last night for the three rooms. As I was totally unaware that you were not a couple, I could see no reason not to let out the three rooms, that is what hotels do." Her voice was mocking.

"Well, we can't share a room can we?" Martin pointed out. "We're not married, or even going out."

"Your relationship issues have nothing to do with me. I have one room reserved for you. Do you want it or not?"

"We'll make do." Susan nodded in the hope that such an arrangement might make for an interesting weekend.

"No Susan, it won't work," Martin sounded forceful, unusual for him.

She leaned in closer to Martin and whispered, "I know about the Windeze tablets, don't be embarrassed if you fart in your sleep."

He sighed loudly, ignored Susan's comment and said to the receptionist, "Is there another hotel around?"

As Martin asked his question in an exasperated tone, a smartly dressed, tall, thin man with a mop of curly red hair, an oval face with eyes topped by thick ginger eyebrows, walked up to Martin, patting him on the back.

"Last to arrive, you must be Martin. Howard has told me all about you." He thrust his hand forward to be shaken. "I'm Henry, Howard's father, pleased to meet you both. Problem?"

Martin briefly explained the predicament and concluded that he would let Susan have the room set aside for him, while he would be happy to find another hotel close by. All the while, he could hear the receptionist tutting softly and impatiently behind him.

"We can't have that, having you billeting off site. Gillian," he addressed the receptionist by her first name as if they were old friends, which they were not, "is there nothing we can do to resolve this situation? I'm sure Martin here, being the gentleman he is, will not be too fussy about where he sleeps, as long as his 'gal' has a comfy bed. What about staff quarters? I know you have some of them." He turned to Martin boasting, "Helped the owner when he was refreshing this place a few years ago. I had contacts in the planning office."

Once again, Gillian annoyed that her authority was being questioned by a friend of her boss, looked at her computer screen. She knew too well that if Henry Phillips was asking for something it was as good as if her boss made the request. Her manager she quite liked, but Henry, well he was another matter altogether. She would not trust him as far as she could throw him. Plus she had heard rumours about him and a shady side of his life that few were comfortable talking about. Such gossip only confirmed her doubts. Nevertheless, she acquiesced to his request, she had little choice.

She flicked her hair back once more, then opened a large red book next to her, ran her finger down a column before announcing, "There's one staff room free until Monday morning." It was a begrudging admission.

"There we go," Henry sounded victorious. "Problem solved, might not be as plush as the paying guest rooms, but if you're anything like my Howard, after a few beers he's not bothered where he lays his head down." Henry turned and walked away, calling out, "See you later tonight in the restaurant."

***

It was not helping Martin in the least, Susan sending him copious WhatsApp messages with photographs of her 'luxury room'. The large double bed, the widescreen television, tea and coffee making facilities, minibar, walk in shower as well as a deep bath. Comments such as 'cool', 'wow', 'brill' were equally contributing to Martin's sense of disappointment in his own room and relief he was not a hotel worker.

The staff bedroom he would describe as a garret, a cramped garret at that. A small dirty window was adjacent to a sagging single bed. The bedside table was a well-worn example with a complex pattern of circles where countless hot cups had been placed. There was a hanging rail loosely attached to the back of the bathroom door, with three mis-shaped wire coat hangers waiting to be utilised. The bathroom was small and grimy with a damp musty odour. Other facilities included a discoloured toilet, a small, cracked hand basin and a shower cubicle that had black mould on the back wall. That was it.

If Martin had a cat to hand, he would not be able to swing it without giving the cat a serious head injury. He consoled himself that it was only for a couple of nights. It could be worse, not a lot, but it could be worse. He looked at his watch, almost time to meet up with the groom in the bar.

Chapter 2

Built in the late nineteenth century, Harby Hall was the country home of a successful merchant and his family. Over time the Midas touch of the family waned, especially when the last family member of the house invested heavily in a South African gold mine that never actually existed. This gave the opportunity for a hotel group to take over the period house and extend the building into the once well-cared-for landscaped gardens. The resulting modern brick-built development was for many locals a wart on the side of the original loved building and should never have been allowed in the first place. Despite local objections, planning permission was approved and the project progressed. There were murmurings of discontent from villagers while the building work was going on. Grumblings that largely went away when the additional jobs the hotel provided brought a new lease of life to the parish and its residents.

The hotel bar made full use of what had once been the family day room. It benefitted from a large fireplace with a sculptured marble surround and a mirror ornately framed above it. The room was full of small tables and comfortable chairs, encouraging residents to relax and drink. It was a light airy room, with a network of plaster freezes decorating the high ceiling. Located on the corner of the building it had two exterior walls, one comprised adjoining tall, glazed doors that in the summer were opened allowing customers to spill out onto the terrace.

A sophisticated, stylish room, totally wasted on Susan whose eyes were firmly fixed on the biceps of the man sitting opposite her. That was when she was not looking at the other man also sitting opposite with an equally impressive physique. She ignored Martin next to her who was, well, just an average bloke in the body department.

They were not, as Susan was imagining, undressed. Both were wearing tight fitting formal white shirts. One had a light jumper draped over his shoulders, the other a scarf casually around his neck. Neither of them needed the extra layer, the garments were just fashion accessories.

"I'm sorry about the bedroom confusion," Howard apologised. "When Martin asked about another bedroom, the hotel told me they had spare rooms. I didn't for one minute imagine that three would go overnight. It wouldn't surprise me if my parents have invited a new raft of relations to the wedding without telling me."

The best man had already been introduced as Neville Maw. He leaned across the table and cupped his hand over Susan's. "Martin missed an opportunity. I would not have given up so easily a chance to share a room with such a beauty." He smiled then drew his hand back.

"The trouble with Martin is that he doesn't know a good thing when he sees it," Susan said impulsively as she felt an uncomfortable flush coming on.

"He doesn't know how to shower either," Neville laughed, then Howard joined in the mockery.

"I wondered how long that might take to be brought up. Rugby players do like to mock others," Martin told Susan.

"Come on, Martin, you must admit showers are your nemesis," said Howard.

"I know about the fall in the shower and the broken tooth, when he tells everyone it was a rugby injury," Susan shared her story.

"Well, it was," Martin protested.

"Technically it was Susan," Howard confirmed with a smile, "the showers were at the rugby club. It was just he was borrowing them to change before going out for the night following an afternoon in the club bar, hence the slip up as we call it.

"I am also willing to bet he has never told you about the Amsterdam shower incident."

Shaking her head, Susan leaned forward in the hope of encouraging the story to be told despite protests from Martin.

"Just ignore Martin," Neville said. "I'll tell you the whole story which began when the team were doing a mini tour of Holland, playing local clubs, staying at the players' homes, a sort of exchange trip for rugby players. I would say that Martin, being a keen supporter of the club, came along to support us. Or was it the temptation of cannabis cafes and red-light districts Martin?"

"Neither, I enjoy rugby," Martin protested.

"Anyway, we arrived at our host's house and were offered the chance to freshen up before dinner. Martin went first, the story is best told from his viewpoint."

"The story is best not told at all."

"Shut up Martin. Carry on Neville," Susan urged for the story to continue.

"Well, Susan, Martin walks into the washing and toilet room, locks the door and looks around. There's no shower cubicle, just a shower jet hanging out of the wall. He sees what I will describe as a large square-shaped plastic bathtub. Martin thinks I can't just shower all over the floor, hence, he drags said plastic bathtub over, half fills it with water, squeezes in and purifies his body, no doubt with scented oils and rose petals."

Martin shrugged at the joke, Susan laughed loudly, sending ripples through the gentle conversations that were being pursued on other tables.

"Once clean, he thinks what do I do with the water? There was a drain set into the floor. I think you know where this is going, don't you Susan?" Neville smiled. "Not content with taking the easy option and just tipping the thing over, he finds a measuring jug and begins to bail out the bathtub, carefully ensuring that the tiled floor does not get too wet. He can be a bit of an old lady at times. You see what's happening here, don't you Susan, you're sophisticated, I can tell."

"It was a wet room with just a shower, I love those, no banging your elbows on the sides." She turned to Martin, "I bet you felt a fool."

"In my defence, at the time I had never seen a wet room in a residential home, I just assumed it was a continental bathroom. It transpired that the large plastic bathtub was for the children. Sadly, I have not lived it down. Now I suppose the next tale will be the inflatable snowman story."

Neville laughed, "I had forgotten that one. I was going to tell Susan about the floating melon in the lake, but I'm happy to include the inflatable snowman if you wish."

With an exasperated look, Martin picked up his beer and leaned back in his chair waiting for the onslaught of excruciatingly embarrassing stories that were coming Susan's way. There was no stopping his so-called mates, once they started it was going to be hard to get them to finish. Martin regretted several things he had done in his life, fortunately none of them had hurt other people, most of them were just humiliating for him.

"I have never been to a rugby match," Susan confessed when they had tired of teasing Martin and his funny eccentricities.

"I'll make a point of inviting you to our next home match as my guest," Neville swiftly offered.

"Oh, that'll be nice."

"I can always take you and at least I'll be on the side lines explaining the game," Martin counter offered.

"That might be so Martin, but you're not one of the players like Neville is." She smiled at him.

"You are detectives I hear. I like ladies in uniform," the tone that Neville used towards Susan was now bluntly flirtatious.

Martin stepped in. "Private detectives, we don't wear uniforms."

Susan was not having any of that. "It can be arranged, the uniform thing I mean, it might be fun."

"Susan," Martin sounded as if he was about to chastise her as though she was his daughter, then thought better of it making his voice softer, "bit too much information."

It was Howard who diplomatically changed the subject, "Detective Martin, still fooling your mother into believing that you're actually working for a living?"

"I think I am succeeding but she is a sly old fox at the best of times. Thanks to Susan's efforts, we do occasionally get involved and detect, it is not all lazing around."

That was Susan's cue to launch into a summary of the cases they had newly solved. In Martin's opinion she did exaggerate some of their detecting skills but that was no surprise to him. Resigning himself to listening, he looked at his watch, he guessed that Howard would soon be winding up this conversation, the three of them had a restaurant meal to prepare for.

***

After polite kisses on both cheeks and warm hugs, Susan left the bar with Martin. She was experiencing a feeling of being attractive and starting to regret not asking the questions she wanted to. Instead, she asked Martin one as they walked through the spacious reception where some residents were having afternoon tea and sandwiches.

"Does Neville have a girlfriend?"

"No, he's married with a new-born son. He has and always will be a natural flirt. He is also intensely loyal and faithful to his wife. Sorry to disappoint you."

"I bet you're pleased, mister green-eyed jealous man; you were getting a little grumpy back there. Secret feelings for me?"

"I was worried that you were getting your hopes up of landing a big burly rugby player, when all the time I knew it was not going to happen. I hate to see you disappointed."

"You can be so sweet Martin. It's rather endearing hiding your emotions and..." Susan stopped talking abruptly, also she stopped walking, tugging at Martin to ensure he stopped alongside her.

"Is that your mother sitting over there?" Susan pointed towards the back of an old lady who was sitting on a long sofa. Martin looked and squinted a little, all he had to go on was an acute angle of the woman's side profile.

"Well, all old ladies look the same to me. It won't be Mother; she likes to stay in the safety of London postcodes and then only certain ones. Come on, I need to get showered and changed before tonight's refined stag party."

"That's your mother. I can't explain it but I'm sure it's her."

They stood and continued to stare at the little old lady as she looked up at the two people who joined her standing in front of her, engaging her in conversation. One was a tall young blonde woman, the other was an older man wearing a neatly styled floral dress. As he calmly glanced up, he caught sight of Martin and Susan. A look of astonishment washed over his face.

"Suzie Baby, is that really you?" Colin called out across the reception, attracting looks from all the guests and staff present.

"Oh God, it is my mother," Martin admitted quietly to himself as Susan dragged him towards the sofa and the familiar faces.

***

Yesterday, Becky had made breakfast for Martin's mother. It was not in her job description; it was just that Becky, the family accountant, was naturally kind and more than happy to help Mother recuperate from her recent stay in hospital. Having heard the mail drop through the letter box Becky ambled along the carpeted hallway to collect it. Yet before reaching the door, she noticed on the hall stand a pamphlet for the Harby Hall Hotel, absently she picked it up and read the narrative.

The resort sounded idyllic, in the countryside, far from the busy capital, peaceful and restful. Becky began to wonder if perhaps a few days away would be good for Martin's mother, assist her recovery. A couple of nights with a change of scenery can be so beneficial, she thought. Forgetting the post on the doormat she returned to the kitchen where Mother was eating porridge with a sliced banana on top.

The immediate response when Becky suggested some nights away would do her good, was entirely negative. It was made clear to Becky that Mother did not like to leave London. The countryside can be confusing and often cold, lacks good public transport, it was not a good place to be. Becky persisted, pointing out that if they went to the Harby Hall Hotel, it being at one time the country home of a well-to-do family, there would be no need to leave the environs of it. Indeed, she could be the lady of the manor for a few nights. Becky hoped she was appealing to the old lady's dominant side. Mother did soften, but then put up the barrier of it being hard to reach the hotel as Becky could not drive. It would mean taking trains and taxis and she was sure that you can't get a genuine black cab outside of London.

Becky, trying to be helpful, pointed out that the hotel was just outside Grantham, only a short cab ride away from the station. She added that many taxi drivers outside of London drive very spacious and comfortable cars. Mother, having finished her porridge, looked at Becky with a thoughtful frown.

"Near Grantham, you say. That is where the great lady was born, Margaret Thatcher, best Prime Minister this country has ever had. I have always wanted to visit the lowly place she was born. No great mansion for her. She lived above her father's shop. It would be nice to see the location for myself, always admired her, but I don't like trains. Can we get a chauffeur to drive us up there and ferry us around?"

"A chauffeur? Isn't that going to cost a fortune?"

"I know you are my accountant and wisely thinking about holding costs down, but a visit to see the birthplace of Margaret Thatcher, why Martin has never suggested that before I have no idea, but such a visit would be worth it, a good distraction."

Becky thought for a few moments. If the old lady was keen to go and wanted to be driven, she had an idea.

"What about Martin's friend Colin? He drives, he's an ex-policeman, he's always willing to lend a hand. Then if we hire a car for the weekend, something more suitable for you, he can drive us around. I know he'll refuse any payment, but we can at least pay for his room which will be a lot cheaper than hiring a genuine chauffeur."

"The famous Broad Street Greengrocers, fancy getting the chance to go and pay homage." Mother was not listening to Becky; in her mind she was preparing to walk on the hallowed ground that Margaret Thatcher once trod.

"Great idea Becky, make it happen. Let's go this weekend whatever the cost, it is time I treated myself in my old age. Never know how long we have on this earth."

It only took a few phone calls. Colin was more than happy to transport them around the countryside of Lincolnshire and suggested leaving the car hire to him. The next telephone call was to the hotel, yes, they had three rooms, the last three rooms left for that weekend. Becky loved it when a plan came together.

***

In hushed tones, Becky divulged to Susan the set of circumstances that led to her choosing the same hotel as where they were staying. With hindsight, Becky admitted that she should have at least paid attention to Martin when he said he was going away for the weekend, carefully noting in her brain where the wedding was being held. She confessed to Susan that as soon as he had mentioned going away, her brain began to imagine a number of scenarios for the weekend, most concluded with Susan sharing a bed with him, which she was informed by Susan had almost happened.

While the girls were talking, Colin was enjoying the spectacle of Martin being chastised by his mother.

"What on earth are you doing here Martin? You are meant to be at a wedding, or have you been lying to your mother, all the while spending a dirty weekend away with your secretary."

"Director, remember Mrs Hayden, she is a director of Hayden Investigations, so he's spending a dirty weekend away with a director," Colin unhelpfully pointed out.

"That might be so, but as Martin's mother I am fully aware that Martin's brain is not always in charge of what his body decides to do. Are you and her sharing a room?"

"No Mother, I find myself in the staff quarters because someone took the last three rooms. Also, I am at a wedding, or will be tomorrow, this is the venue for it. Howard and Hanna are getting married in the hotel garden."

"Whatever is wrong with young people these days? What's so terrible with a church wedding, they have served us all for centuries, but the younger generation have to change everything. One other thing, did you know that your friend Coleen likes to dress up in women's clothes?"

She asked the question, unconcerned that Colin was standing next to her.

"Yes Mother, I do. And his name is Colin. Forgive me for asking, I know you have only just arrived, but when are you planning to depart?"

"Monday morning. Becky and I have planned a very useful itinerary and Coleen here is being kind enough to drive us around and then take us back to London. The sort of thing a son should be doing for his mother."

"Every time I suggested a weekend in the country, you refused out of hand."

"Ah yes," Colin mischievously butted in, "but you didn't offer your mother the chance to see Margaret Thatcher's birthplace, did you? And we all know what a draw that is. Think of the great names of history and their hometowns, Stratford upon Avon, Blenheim Palace, Grantham, Croydon, they all just roll off the tongue."

"Not only is Coleen a transvestite, I think they are called that, but he is also very denigrating at times," Mother pointed out, no one else was surprised. "Well, once we have settled in, we are all having dinner together. Martin and Susan, I trust you will be joining us."

"No Mother, I am going for a meal with the groom and his father. Susan might be able to join you, what do you think, Susan?"

"Ah, I would love to join you but," she paused, trying to think of an excuse, "I am walking the town tonight; the streetlights are very different in design to others in the county. Quite interesting in their own way."

"Really?" Colin asked, knowing full well that Susan was lying.

"Well, if not tonight, then, as you have the wedding tomorrow, I insist that Sunday night my son, and you Susan join us for dinner. I will not hear a word against it. Now Becky, let's go upstairs and we will get ourselves unpacked. I hate my clothes being folded too long in the suitcase. Coleen, be a dear and bring up our cases."

"Being a dear is what I do best M'lady," Colin replied as he picked up the cases, winking at Martin.

"See what I mean Martin, mockery and poor fashion sense, like so many of your friends," Mother said as she walked off with Becky.

Chapter 3

Just how Martin had ended up sitting next to an elderly man called Mr Stewart and opposite Henry Phillips, the groom's father, he was not sure. Arriving late might have contributed to the placement. All he did know was that he was well away from the groom, the best man and the other rugby players at the other end of the long table, all of whom appeared to be having much more fun than him.

A succession of banal anecdotes flowed from Henry's tongue. Like the fact his father had given him his name to ensure the initials HP followed him around. For the same reason he called his own son Howard, continuing the theme which pointed, allegedly, to the fact that the family were a saucy bunch. Martin was mildly amused out of a sense of politeness, as he had already heard from Howard of this strange family tradition.

Henry was beside himself with glee that his son was marrying Hanna and was hoping that they would, in the fullness of time, be presenting a grandchild to him with a name beginning with 'H'.

Mr Stewart also laughed politely; no doubt having heard the story many times. Martin just smiled then struck up a conversation with Edwin Stewart to avoid another butcher story from Mr Phillips, who Martin had learned over the last boring hour owned a chain of butchers across the county called, 'Phillips Fillets." Clearly the family had a warped sense of names.

Edwin Stewart was an old man, the oldest in the room by at least two decades in Martin's guesstimate. He was also an oddball, of that Martin was certain. Apart from red corduroy trousers, a checked shirt under a padded gilet, he was also wearing a black homburg hat. The hat and gilet he continued to wear throughout the meal. In the band of the hat was a large black and white feather, which Edwin proudly pointed out was a feather from a Great Spotted Woodpecker, or to use its Latin name, Dendrocopos major. Martin wondered what it was about Grantham people and names.

If Edwin's dress sense was odd, then his dietary requirements were simply bizarre. He had brought his own food to the restaurant. An ASDA ready meal, which the restaurant kitchen seemed happy to microwave and serve on a plate. During the course of the evening, Martin learnt that it was Mr Phillips's universal influence in all matters relating to business that allowed such an event to take place. "Good contacts in the Chamber of Commerce," he proudly told Martin. Clearly, Henry Phillips was the Mr Fixit of Grantham.

Curiosity got the better of Martin as he watched Edwin tuck into his meal, which had not even been turned out onto a plate, it was still in the microwavable plastic container it was sold in.

"Why did you bring your own food to this restaurant? I can promise you this tagliatelle is delectable."

"That might be so young man," Edwin replied, carefully putting his knife and fork down. Turning to Martin with a small strip of pasta still adhering to his wrinkled lip, he explained, "I just like to know what I am getting, and consistency is something I treasure. Take your Salmon and Pea Tagliatelle, it might be nice here, yet if you toddle off to another Italian restaurant and order the same thing, the ratio of peas to salmon will vary, depending on how much profit the owners want to make. Then the taste will be different with cheaper ingredients. Why go to a restaurant and be disappointed? I bring my own, this ASDA Chicken Tagliatelle arrives out of the microwave the same every time. No surprises for me, that is how I like it. I would add, just to be clear, I rarely go out anymore. I live on my own, so a selection of microwaveable meals designed for one person are ideal for my meagre requirements."

Martin could not deny there was a certain logic to Edwin's flamboyant eating habits. Plus a part of him was envious that with age comes the ability to do whatever you want.

"May I ask you Edwin, how you are related to the family?"

"What you mean is why is an old fogey like me joining with the young ones in their pre-nuptial celebrations. Howard is my godson. I've known the family for years. Like Henry, I, many years ago, owned a small shop selling antiques. I do wish to point out, not a crass second-hand shop trading above its station, my shop was a real antiques shop with genuine treasures to be found within. I specialised in coins, bank notes, postcards, medals, all small objects created a bigger turnover. Much more likely to get an impulse buyer for a ten-shilling note than a Chippendale chair."

At this point, Martin felt his mobile phone vibrate. A notification. He apologised, then took the phone out and looked at the message. It was Susan.

'I have a problem and need your help when you get back come to my room whatever time we need to speak x'

"What is it with young people who think that just because you are using a phone, grammar is not important," Edwin commented, having leant towards Martin to read the message.

"This is a private message you know." Martin felt a tinge of anger.

"Then you should shield it. Holding it in front of you like that is as good as sharing it. Are you going?"

"I'll pop in and see her when I leave here."

"Could be important."

"Knowing Susan, it'll be important only to her."

"I don't know young man, women need to be humoured." Edwin looked down the table toward his godson, then called out with a power beyond the appearance of an old man, "Howard, your friend here is needed by a woman called Susan in her room. I think he should be released from his social obligations at this peaceful event."

A silence fell across the table and rippled beyond the restaurant. Eyes stared at Martin before Howard replied, "Martin, if your Susan needs you in her room, you had best go. You can't deny the needs of a young woman, you crafty old fox."

"It's nothing like that. She has a problem and needs to chat."

"Martin," Howard continued from the other end of the table, as the other guests listened intently, "you can call it a chat if you want. No need to be ashamed, you're amongst friends. I saw how jealous you were getting when Neville here was flirting with her. Best get going if she needs a man!"

That brought a bout of ridiculing laughter from the party, as well as a collection of colourful comments worthy of any rugby team. If it had been anyone else asking for help with a problem, Martin would have stayed but it was Susan, and what Edwin had said he could not deny, she really could need help. He left the restaurant with an assortment of banter and laughter ringing in his ears.

***

The door opened. Susan looked furtive as she checked the corridor before urging Martin quickly into the room. He glanced around; it appeared tidy in a Susan sort of way. She seemed to be uninjured and sober, he was mystified.

The room was as grand as it had appeared in the photographs she had sent Martin earlier. He imagined that his cramped staff room would fit into the wardrobe of this room. He put his envy to one side and asked, "What is this problem you have?"

"In there." Susan pointed towards the closed door of the bathroom.

"Susan, if there is a problem with the plumbing, then you can call reception and they will be able to deal with it a lot better than I can."

"It's not plumbing. It's in there."

"What is it?" Martin began to sound a little irritated.

"Just look."

Exasperated he opened the door whilst holding his breath, never sure what sort of odours the room might have.

He did not see it at first, it was too small as he looked around at eye level. He felt a pawing at his leg, scratching at his trousers, he looked down.

"A dog. Susan, why do you have a dog in your bathroom?" Martin picked up the small, excited Yorkshire Terrier, which desperately wanted to lick his cheeks. He was having none of that, so he held the dog at arm's length.

"Sit down and I'll tell you." Susan patted the bed cover, indicating that Martin should sit next to her.

"You know I said to your mother I was going walkabout looking at lamp posts."

"Yes, but I knew you were lying."

"At the time, yes, then I felt guilty so I thought I would pop out and have a look at some, so technically I wasn't lying to your mother."

"I suppose that makes Susan sense. How were they, the lamp posts, I mean?"

"Boring. But when I was out this little fellow came bounding up to me and wanted to be friends. He's sweet, isn't he? I couldn't see any owner nearby. Clearly, he had escaped from somewhere. On his collar he has a tag with his name and the address of his owner."

Martin looked at the brass disc attached to the dog's collar. "Jupiter, that's an odd name for a small dog."

"I thought so too. Anyway, I asked a few locals and they directed me to the address, which is no more than a burnt-out shell of a house. A detached house, all blackened and empty, no-one living there. There's a neighbour on one side, so I rang their bell, but no answer. On the other side of the burnt-out house is a church that's closed and empty. There were some other houses on that street, but it was getting dark and late and I thought it best to go back in the morning, then you can come with me. We can knock on lots more doors and hopefully find whoever owns Jupiter."

"If you're going back in the morning, with or without me, then why the text?"

"You didn't have to come running, it wasn't urgent. How was the meal?"

"I thought you might be in trouble, that's why I came rushing to your room."

"Ah, my knight in shining armour, you're so sweet at times."

"Okay, I'll leave you and Jupiter here to spend the night together and I'll see you at breakfast. Oh, when you do come down in the morning, leave the 'do not disturb' sign on your door, dogs are not allowed in this hotel."

Martin walked along the corridor towards the staff quarters. It had been a tiring day; he was looking forward to a refreshing shower and then a good night's sleep. If he had known what was waiting for him, he might well have decided to sleep on Susan's bathroom floor with Jupiter.

***

It was just before eleven when Colin sat at the hotel bar savouring a refreshing Cinzano and tonic, lots of ice and a slice of lemon. He was alone at the bar. The only other customers were a young couple chatting quietly at a small round table not too far away. From his high stool, he could look into the day room where most of the tables were located, three of which were occupied. It was all very serene.

He was not so much tired, more relieved that Becky and Mother had now retired to their respective bedrooms. He could relax without Mother asking questions like, 'Did your mother dress you as a little girl when you were young?' or 'Which toilets do you use?' Not that he was concerned what she or anyone else thought, Colin was Colin, you took him as you found him. At least the barmaid asked him practical questions.

"Don't you find it difficult to get up on a bar stool in a pencil dress?" she asked as she dreamily polished a wine glass.

"My dear, as a man in a woman's clothes, nothing is practical in this world for you or me. The world I have learnt has been designed by men for men who dress in men's clothes. Escalators I find a nightmare in high heels forcing me to wear sensible flats when I go shopping. Just so unfair."

The barmaid was a large woman in her fifties. You could not describe her as fat, in her own words, just lumpy. She had big blue eyes, which she had surrounded with deep blue eyeshadow and dark blue mascara. She had a small mouth with big lips. Colin was not going to ask, but he suspected she had had a Botox injection in the lips. As she wiped the bar with a cloth, he noticed the rings she wore on her fingers, one on each little finger, a wedding band, plus one on each index finger, in Colin's eyes that was a lot of bling.

"You're wearing some very attractive rings, expensive looking. I hope all the bar work doesn't hurt them."

She splayed her hands out, displaying the golden rings as if she was a peacock.

"I have never been one for jewellery, but it just so happens my husband has a small jewellery shop. I think he looks upon me as a sort of shop window."

Colin laughed and offered to buy her a drink.

"We can't drink on duty, but thanks anyway."

"Quiet night tonight?"

"Yes, calm before the storm tomorrow. Weddings are a case of all hands on deck, especially as I understand most of the guests are rugby players, they do have a reputation, I know from previous experience. Plus, the father of the groom is well known around these parts for all the wrong reasons."

"You intrigue me, 'wrong reasons', what might they be?"

"Well, I shouldn't say too much, depends which side of the fence you are on. Our boss, as do most businessmen in the area, adore him. They hold their Chamber of Commerce meetings here every month. But there are rumours and gossip that taint his halo."

"I'm on the side of the fence where the gossip is; can you enlighten me?"

"Well," she leaned closer to him, "there was the story of the launderette. I have heard," she stopped and looked up. "Ah, look a latecomer and one of the wedding guests," she nodded towards the man walking towards the bar. "I'll tell you another time."

Colin looked around to see who the guest was.

"Martin my love, what are you doing here?"

Martin perched himself on the stool next to Colin and ordered a double brandy for himself, a Cinzano and tonic for Colin, the barmaid turned down the offer of a drink.

"What am I doing here," Martin said wearily. "I'm starting to regret ever inviting Susan to come along to this wedding weekend. And now berating myself for not hiding the hotel brochure from Becky. Lastly, I'm planning to spend the night on one of those comfy looking chairs in the day room. Let me explain."

***

The narrow corridors of the staff quarters had never been carpeted, no such luxury was afforded for the hotel employees, instead it had just a plain wooden flooring that echoed Martin's footsteps. As he walked, he began to think about Mother, not in a caring way, more as a puzzle he was trying to work out.

Since his father had died, she had shown no interest in being away from her house. Often he had suggested a few days by the coast, pointing out how good it was to have a change of surroundings. Every offer he had made was rejected. It was not only her reluctance to have a holiday, but she was also very careful with money, only buying clothes as a last resort, preferring the cheaper cuts of meat, and wearing a disapproving look whenever he brought anything new into the house.

Now Mother was here at a hotel in Lincolnshire, paying for three rooms, no doubt including meals. She had also hired a large prestigious car for the weekend. Martin would not have believed it, had he not heard the facts from Becky via Susan. Did she have a warped plan at the back of her mind that would only become apparent when it was too late?

As Martin twisted the key to unlock his room, he tried to square this circle of confusion. He heard the unmistakable noise of two passionate people in a nearby room enjoying each other's company a little too much. He became aware he was correct in his assumption as he stepped through the doorway, but he had been wrong about it being in another room. The noises were coming from his single bed. A racket was emitting from under an off-white sheet that was shifting as if it was caught in a gale-force wind. Martin stood and stared, not sure exactly what the social protocol might be in such a circumstance.

To be sure, Martin looked around the cramped noisy room. His case was just where he had left it; without a doubt this was his room. Now he knew what the three bears must have thought, although thankfully for the protection of innocent children around the world, Goldilocks was only sleeping.

The sheets stopped moving and a large red-faced man appeared from under the sheets and inspected Martin with a curious look.

"Who are you mate?" the large man sounded breathless. An equally flushed female face appeared from under him.

"The occupant of this room," Martin pointed out wrongly. He was more of a guest, paying too much for a small shabby room that now appeared to be used by random people for sex.

"Shit, you're a paying guest, aren't you? And 'cause of this bloody wedding they've used my room 'cause they've run out of rooms. Bloody hopeless reception staff."

"You say your room, which therefore must make you staff?"

"Yeah, late finishes and early starts we get a room. Only to ensure we're here to do breakfast and stuff, the bosses ain't a charity. When I'm having a day off this room is normally empty and I can make the best use of it, as you can see. Look mate, can you do me a favour? Give me an hour or so and I'll be out, promise, then it's all yours. Well, until Monday lunchtime when I'm back to work."

Respectfully and a little stunned Martin left the room closing the door behind him, wondering if anything about this wedding weekend was going to be a pleasure.

***

"Sounds to me like you're using Andy's room," the barmaid explained having listened closely to Martin's experience. "Randy git, always chasing women. Sorry you had to encounter such a sight. Have the drinks on the house, sort of compensation for having to witness Andy at play."

"Why can't he do that sort of thing in his own home?" Martin innocently asked.

"As nice as she might be, I don't think his wife would approve of Andy bringing home casual women to have it off with."

"Married, hence the vacant room is too good an asset to miss out on," Martin commented as he downed the brandy in one.

"Going back to my original question," Colin was curious, "why on earth do you regret inviting Susan to this weekend?"

"She has, in her own special way, found a stray dog and wants to reunite it with its owner. Although she says I have a choice to help her in the morning, you know, and I know that is not an option Susan hands out often. The yappy little terrier gets to share her luxury room while I get to sleep on a sofa over there. Where's the justice in that?" Martin looked at the barmaid who was listening to the story. "You didn't hear that, did you?"

"I have no interest in what happens anywhere else in the hotel, the bar is my domain. Carry on," she replied with a tired edge to her voice.

"Well, just keep your fingers crossed that Susan does not lead you into some tangled investigation, you know what she's like for getting involved."

"I plan to avoid any form of investigation this weekend, which is why I want to avoid trying to find the owner."

The barmaid leaned onto the bar closer to the two men. "Investigations you say, are you police officers?"

"No dear," Colin replied, "Martin here is a private detective. I help out now and again with his inquiries."

"Do you charge much?" the barmaid asked Martin.

Colin responded on his behalf, "Martin is a detective who avoids detecting at all costs. He has enough money in the family fortune to allow him to do nothing at all at the office all day. The point of this so-called work is to satisfy his mother's strict instructions that he must have a worthwhile job. It's extremely complex, but from your point of view he mostly works for nothing. Why do you ask?"

"I think my husband is having an affair. I would like to hire a private detective to follow him, see what he's up to."

"Really this is a social weekend for me, not too enjoyable at the present time, but nevertheless a work break." Martin began to rub his earlobe. Part of him felt a little uncaring, turning her down, she was obviously concerned about her husband and being fully aware of Andy and his antics, well Martin could empathise with her. But helping was a step too far.

Colin pursued the conversation, "Just why do you think he's having an affair, sorry, I don't know your name."

"Imogen. He goes out every Sunday night. He knows I always work Saturday and Sunday nights and when I get back, he smells of a woman's perfume. I have asked him about it, but he just says there are some women at the bar he goes to with his friends. The thing is I often smell the same perfume on him at other times during the week, when he has been at work."

"Imogen please don't take this the wrong way," Colin was being tentative, an unusual mannerism for him Martin thought, "but could it be that your husband and his friends are a little like me, enjoying the feel of wearing female clothing?"

"Well, to be honest I never thought of that, but I don't think so."

"We need to touch all bases. You say every Sunday night he goes out, so tomorrow it will be the same?"

"Yes, regular as clockwork. I know he leaves at six in the evening, my neighbour has told me."

"In that case, I am sure my friend Martin here would be happy to take on the case for you and answer those burning questions you have. We just need to know your address and leave the rest to us Imogen."

She beamed and turned to the back of the bar to look for pen and paper. Unsurprisingly, Martin was a little confused and expressed his feelings to Colin.

"Colin," he whispered, out of earshot of Imogen who had now moved to the other end of the bar still searching out some writing materials. "I just said I am having a social weekend, no work. In fact, that is, as you very well know, always my raison d'etre. Why are you volunteering me? Are you standing in for Susan as she is absent from the conversation?"

"Let me point out a couple of things which might help you reconsider and in fact enthuse you into helping poor Imogen, who, between you and me, I think has had a little cosmetic work on her face to wipe away the years. Clearly, that's failed, but full marks for trying.

"Anyway, that's beside the point, except to prove she's desperate to keep her husband. Now she wants you to follow her husband all Sunday evening, not a burdensome task. I imagine you will track him to some bar, he'll meet a woman, they'll have a drink before going to a discreet location to do whatever they want to do. Then you can come back here for a drink with Imogen and share the results of your persistent endeavours.

"Now what if you turn down this opportunity? The alternative version of your Sunday evening will be dinner with a certain Mrs Hayden, you know, your mother. I think I can guess which opportunity you will be choosing on Sunday night." Colin grinned; he had no need to wait for an answer.

When Imogen returned, she handed her address to Martin and gave him a brief description of her husband, said she would be eternally grateful to him when he confirmed that there would be no charge, because he would be happy to do it as a favour.

Colin did ask, "What were you saying about the groom's father?"

Imogen coyly looked at Martin and then back to Colin. "Maybe another time."

"Fair enough. Finally young man," Colin patted Martin's hand, "knowing you so well I presume you will not be going back to your humble room to sleep on still warm and possibly damp sheets. Can I offer you the hospitality of chez nous? I have a spare single bed in my room, which I am sure will be a lot more comfortable than one of those sofas over there?"

With a friendly slap on Colin's back Martin smiled. "I'll get my case. You do know me too well."

Chapter 4

"There is really no need for me to be here," Martin complained, pulling an enthusiastic Jupiter away from a rusty dented lamp post the dog was surveying as he prepared to pee over it.

Susan, who was walking a little in front of Martin, turned to look him in the eye, holding her hands on her hips. She reminded Martin of one of his teachers at boarding school, a lot more attractive, but equally angry.

"I'm not asking you to sacrifice your life for me, just to accompany me in the duty of returning this dog to its rightful owner. I know the street can't be far away."

Dutifully Martin followed, pulling Jupiter along with him. Things would have been a lot easier if Jupiter still had that sweet little disc around his neck revealing the little fellow's address, but sadly, that was no longer the case. For some reason late last night Susan thought it a good idea to give the little terrier a shower. She explained how it had not been easy holding the dog under the shower head, lathering him up. Martin pointed out that he might have a fear of drowning. In the ensuing struggle between Susan and Jupiter, the sweet little disc with the postcode fell off his collar, bouncing away unnoticed and presumably lost down the defective plug hole, or at least that was Susan's best guess. Whatever the fate of the brass disc, it was never recovered. The dog was clean and now accompanying two lost humans.

They were looking for a road, which Susan was pretty sure began with C-R-A, but certainly it had a burnt-out house next to a church. Martin hoped as he followed Susan that burnt-out houses next to churches was not a common occurrence in this town on the outskirts of Grantham.

"The trouble is things look so different in the daylight," Susan pointed out as she stood at a crossroads, deciding which route to take next. "I was here last night. I know because of that streetlamp with a deflated rubber ring over it, I'd love to know how it got there. Anyway, I just can't remember if I came from this direction, or from one of the other roads."

The two humans were on the edge of admitting they were lost when the canine member of the trio started yapping and pulling Martin towards the right-hand road. The humans looked at each other and without a word they both knew the dog had a better sense of direction. He led them past a Chinese takeaway, across the forecourt of a Shell garage, then past a dubious looking greengrocer's stall, where he decided to pause briefly to leave his mark on a crate of bananas, which should not have been on the pavement in the first place. After that the dog turned left, closely followed by another left, at which time Susan pointed to the road sign, with an excited pitch in her voice, "Branston Road. That's the road!"

It was indeed the road. At the far end of Branston Road, the tall church spire dominated the corner. Prior to arriving at the church was a burnt-out house. Little Jupiter was by now yapping excitedly, there could be little doubt that the ruins were once his home. The three of them stood in front of the derelict house, marvelling at the blackened brickwork, the charred rafters and the pile of burnt furniture and belongings that lay strewn across the garden. No doubt before the fire the house would have been considered prestigious.

Martin was keen to point out, unkindly, "I thought you said it started with CRA?"

"Pretty sure, I said, it was dark last night and if you are aware, B is next to C in the alphabet, which in my book means I was correct enough."

"How can you be correct enough?" Martin asked the question limply.

"I'm a woman, anything near correct is enough for men to accept we are totally right. We'll try next door first, then work our way down the street," Susan instructed, indicating the row of semi-detached houses and elegant bungalows they had walked past to get to the fire-damaged house. Martin was not so sure about that plan as he held Jupiter back, who seemed overeager to get into the ruined house.

"Let's look around here first."

Martin, encouraged by Jupiter, opened the wooden five-bar gate which was hanging off its hinges and walked across the weed-covered gravel towards the house. He stopped beside a charred coffee table that was discarded upside down on the muddy lawn. A small object caught his eye. He bent down and picked up a small metal disc and examined it.

"It's some sort of medallion or an old coin," Martin decided, although the head on the back of the coin looked a bit like a Roman emperor. He was tempted to throw it back onto the ground, after all it wasn't his. Then he thought it might belong to Jupiter's owner, so he slipped it into his pocket and moved closer to the house. Susan was by this time, standing in front of one of the downstairs voids that had once been a window. She was looking into the main living room of the house, now just a charred space containing a melted television, charred fragments across the floor and a settee, which was now just a maze of springs.

"Have a look at this in the back garden, there's a caravan," Martin called to Susan.

They stood looking at the white caravan with a broad red stripe running around the roof line. Susan, as a child spent time holidaying in caravans, estimated it was a six berth, a decent size. Leaning against the caravan, close to the door was a moped. On the other side of the door were several plastic containers the size of rain butts, some with garden tools protruding from the top. Another contained worn-out umbrellas, plus a tired looking Union Jack flag hanging down. There was also an overflowing rubbish wheelie bin, a crate full of empty beer bottles and two planters, each with four dead plants, brown and withered. A petrol generator purred away at the front, with a power cable disappearing into the caravan through a hole stuffed with plastic bags. The caravan was home to someone, and that someone Jupiter was eager to get to, pulling hard on the lead.

In response to Martin's knocking the door was opened. A large man appeared; his rounded chin was populated by dark stubble of varying depths across his face. His hair, long, untidy and unwashed, hung over his ears. A gap had formed between his sweatshirt and jogging bottoms exposing his belly button and an excessive amount of flesh.

"Jupee! I was so worried, where have you been, you naughty little boy?" The man bent down and Jupiter jumped into his arms and started abundantly licking the cheek of his master. It would have been a heart-warming sight, but for the fact that Martin had just trodden in a dog turd. He surreptitiously tried to wipe his sole clean on the grass, he hoped he was succeeding.

"Where was the little urchin?" the owner asked, hugging a tail-wagging Jupiter.

"I found him last night a few streets away. I did find your house but didn't see the caravan out here in the back garden. We had a good night together; I've looked after him and fed him well."

"Well come in for a sec, this calls for a celebration drink."

It might have been a six-berth caravan, but even so it was difficult for Martin and Susan to find anywhere to sit. Jupiter's owner introduced himself as Rodney. He scurried around removing a pile of dog-eared magazines from one chair. Then for Susan, he cleared a space on a cushioned chair by moving a half-eaten bowl of cornflakes and a remote control, as well as a multi-pack of crisps. After placing Jupiter down, he took three bottles of beer from the fridge, took off the caps and handed one to each guest.

"Cheers guys!" Rodney raised his bottle. "Can't tell you how pleased I am to see my little mate. I let him out yesterday for his afternoon stroll round the garden. He normally has a pee and a shit then comes back in. Dunno what happened, but was a while later I thought to myself, where's little Jupee. That's my nickname for him. Called and searched around the garden but he was nowhere to be seen. I thought give it a day or so, he does like to chase some of the foxes that hang around here. I was getting ready to do some posters, you know, lost dog, picture, that sort of thing and stick 'em on lamp posts around here. But no need now is there you little scamp?" Rodney ruffled the little dog's back, who swiftly laid down and turned over to let his master stroke his tummy.

"Is that your house? The one all burnt out?" Susan nodded towards the window and the blackened brickwork of the building.

"Yeah, well it was my mum's house really. I lived with her for years before she passed away last Christmas. I couldn't ever afford such a place. I'm a bus driver and even with as much overtime as I can grab, I'd never make enough for a mortgage on a house like that, but it's all mine now she's passed on. Thanks Mum." He looked up at the ceiling and raised his bottle in respect of his departed parent.

"Now I suppose you have to wait ages for the insurance company to pay out?" Susan was again the one asking questions. Martin, on the other hand, knew that the less questions they asked the less they would know and as a consequence the less they would care about Rodney.

"Insurance company? Thieving bastards they are. Don't think they're ever going to pay out, they reckon I did it myself. I ask you, why would I burn down my own house? I told them what happened, but they don't believe me. How do I fight my corner, stuck here in a mobile home without a lot of money to fight them with?"

"What happened, an electrical fault?"

"I wish, that would have been easy to prove. It was the church next door; they burnt the house down with their prayers. I can tell you they have it in for me. But apparently, according to the insurance company, the power of prayer does not cause fires. What a bunch of atheists they are."

"Sorry." Just why he was apologising Martin was not entirely sure. He had only had two mouthfuls of beer; he was not hung over, so he must have heard correctly. All the same he thought it was worth checking. "You are saying the church next door burnt your house down by praying?"

"That's about it. Let me explain a little more about the bunch of charlatans next door. To be honest, I was once a member of that church, but they decided that I was bringing them bad luck, I ask you. I was cast out and banned from their services. If that wasn't enough, I caught them doing their mumbo jumbo stuff near my bike. Next day the damn thing wouldn't start. They had cursed it.

"Next, I saw a couple of them waiting at a bus stop. They never got on my bus, just watched me stop, I bet they said a few prayers under their breaths and then I drive off. Ten minutes later, the bus overheats, leaky radiator, steam coming out of everywhere. The passengers must get off and wait for a replacement bus. How I cursed them, the church, not the customers.

"I was doing overtime, late turn. Then I get a call from the police; my house is on fire. Everything just about gone, it looks a lot worse than it really is, the upstairs is all smoke and water damage, the downstairs front is where it's totally gutted. Luckily, I had a caravan which I had recently bought, I was planning to rent a plot by the seaside at Skeggy. I've no proof, but I reckon they were praying that my house burnt down. It was them, hundred percent."

Susan and Martin looked at each other, just to confirm that they had heard the same thing. Susan asked, "Let's get this right. The church thought you were bringing them bad luck and as a consequence they prayed and burnt your house down. Seems a bit harsh."

"There's more to it than that, but they'll never admit it. I know because I used to be part of them. They want to buy this plot of land, knock my house down and build a new temple. They've even got themselves outline planning permission for it. That's the real reason they wanted my property, which no one admits to, and the insurance company just won't listen to me."

"If it was not the power of prayer," Martin said, "does the insurance company know how the fire started?"

"They said it was a couple of candles that I had left burning, bit of a shrine to my mum. But that couldn't have been the cause as I hadn't lit the candles that day. I only light them on a Monday, which was the day of the week that she died."

***

Having turned down the offer of another bottle of beer, they left Jupiter and Rodney celebrating their reunion. As they returned to the road, Susan insisted that it would be the right thing to pop along to the church and have a word. If they wanted to buy Rodney's property, that would have been a strong motive to burn down a house. Susan added that even some clerics are not averse to breaking the law to further their religion.

"I am not sure that I want to upset the house of God, it could lead to difficulties when I get to the end of my life," Martin pointed out to deflect Susan from her proposed path.

Rightly, Martin thought, he had further pointed out that it was really none of their business and that they also had a wedding to attend. The argument was dismissed by Susan as irrelevant. Just a few questions, she said, let them know some detectives are interested in the case, it might be enough to spook them into making errors.

"I'm putting my foot down," Martin told Susan, as he stood motionless on the pavement in the shadow of the church. "I'm the boss, we are not going in there. We are going back to the hotel, get changed and celebrate Howard's wedding."

"Don't forget, I'm a director just like you. Plus, I'm a woman, as I have previously pointed out on numerous occasions, I am always right. Come on, the door's ajar, let's find someone to talk to."

***

The church, occupying a large area, was located on the corner of Branston Street. There was only a small ribbon of grass between the church and the burnt-out house belonging to Rodney.

Susan was not an expert on churches or religion for that matter, having done her best to avoid anything to do with God and Jesus when she was a teenager. To her the building was your average Church of England place of worship with a tall square tower, no doubt with bells. The double doored wooden entrance was shaped like an arch.

St Andrews, as it used to be known, was very much a typical English church. Built around the early nineteen hundreds, it was plain. It aimed to ensure the local flock were pious and without sin. When it opened, the pews were full and the singing was loud but as time went on, the congregation waned. The vicar during the seventies had been defrocked for offering LSD to some of his female flock. After that episode, the church had a reputation which ensured the very religious members of the community found other places to worship. Vicars the church wanted to hide in the shadows were given to St Andrews to see out their careers or take the hint and hang up their dog-collars. Finally, the church building and the land had been sold three years ago.

Everyone expected the church to be converted into odd-shaped flats or some weird furniture showroom, in the end neither happened.

Susan pushed open the arched door and was taken aback by what she saw. There were no pews, no font to be seen and the altar was nothing like the altars she recalled from her younger days. The interior was expansive yet almost empty, but for a floor with a mosaic design which she could not make out precisely. On the floor was a row of oil lamps that burned and flickered in the breeze from the open door. The lamps created a wide corridor leading towards a large statue of a bearded man on a throne. To one side of him was an eagle and in his right hand he held a sceptre in the shape of a lightning bolt. To the left of the statue, which was at least three metres tall, was a young man, tall and lanky, carefully sweeping the floor. He looked up at the visitors with curiosity as he continued to brush the floor.

"Can I help you?" His voice echoed around the space. As with many churches the acoustics were superb, aided by the emptiness of what could pass for a classy dance hall.

"We are looking for the vicar of this church," Martin replied, as both he and Susan walked towards the lanky cleaner. Their steps echoed off the walls, emphasizing the vacuity of the space.

"I think you mean the senator."

"Senator?" Martin repeated. "We are not in America, are we? I want to speak to the person who manages this church, normally in a C of E church that is the vicar."

"A vicar, you think. Tell me who do you think this big statue is of?" The lanky cleaner had now stopped brushing the floor nodding his head towards the big figure on the throne.

"I have no idea," Martin confessed. It was unlike any figurine he had seen in a church. "An old version of Jesus, or God?"

"Well, he is a God, but not your Christian God. This fine fellow, carved out of stone, is Jupiter, King of all Roman Gods, God of the sky and thunder. Before you ask your next question, which will be, 'why is he in a church?', the answer is this is not a church. It's a temple dedicated to Jupiter, somewhere for us mere mortals to praise him and seek his guidance and forgiveness."

"I suppose you all dress up in togas and stuff?" Susan's question was flippant as she could not imagine anyone in modern day England worshipping an ancient Roman god that she had heard of way back in junior school. She had an interest in the Romans, often dreamt of spending her honeymoon touring the ancient sites in Italy, but worshipping?

"Actually, we do." His pronunciation reflected the affront the lanky cleaner felt. "Gods come in all shapes and sizes. It's having the freedom to worship whatever God you wish that's important. I pledge my allegiance to Jupiter and his children and a part of that is to wear the traditional dress of the Roman Empire. You can kneel before whichever deity you wish; I don't care."

"But you're in jeans and a baggy jumper, I know that's not what the Romans wore."

"Let me explain a little more about what we do here." The lanky cleaner leant the broom against a painted pillar, folded his arms and began his explanation. The description was detailed and serious. He introduced himself as Leon Driscoll, whose position within the church was that of a pleb, one of the lowest in the structure, yet that did not bother him in the slightest. He carried out menial tasks around the church, served others during meetings then during worship he would be very much on the side-lines. He saw the look on Susan's face. Then continued to point out that he enjoyed such a position, it was after all not his full-time job. It was no more than a hobby. A hobby he found refreshing and relaxing, a contrast to his day job in computer programming, leading a team of ten programmers, who between them created voice software for large multi-national companies. A hard, stressful job with long hours, it was high pay with high pressure.

"Cleaning the floors is a lesser task that I actually enjoy. I assume that the two of you have not come to join our ranks."

"No Leon," Martin answered, "we're here about the owner of the house next door. He is accusing your church, sorry temple, of burning down his house. We would like to ask a few questions."

"Ah, the plonker next door, or should I say Rodders. Did you know his dad named him after the bloke in *Only Fools and Horses*. He's an odd bloke, used to join us for worship, but then walked out one day. If you're asking about him and any accusation he might have, then you had better speak to our senator. I'll give you his phone number, he'll be able to tell you a lot more than me, a mere pleb." His last comment he pointedly aimed at Susan.

Once outside Martin instructed Susan firmly, "Don't even think about going to see this senator fellow. We have a wedding to go to and I do not intend to miss it to help a group of pseudo-Romans settle their disagreements."

Chapter 5

When Mr Sayers built the original Harby Hall, on the proposed site there was already a sixteenth century manor house which he demolished without a second thought. Mr Sayers always got what he wanted. His destructive eye fortunately did not extend as far as the walled garden, which he kept with its thatched summer house. The reason he kept the walled garden was he valued his privacy and it allowed him his secret indulgence of laying naked on the lawn and feeling the warm rays of the sun on his skin. Partly credited with bringing nudism to the UK, he died young from what we now know is severe skin cancer. Sadly, for Mr Sayers sun-tan lotion had yet to be invented.

Today he would be rushing to grab his underpants as Hanna, soon to be Mrs Phillips, walked towards the thatched summer house arm in arm with her father. On either side of her, guests looked in admiration at the bride, some using their phones to take photographs of her.

On both sides of her were rows of ornate chairs, with a white ribbon draped over the chair back. Every row contained six chairs and there were ten rows on both sides of her. To calm her nerves, Hanna counted each row, 'eight, seven, six,' as she progressed towards the summer house and her husband-to-be. She imagined she was doing the countdown for a rocket launch. Hanna smiled as she heard a recording of Ed Sheeran singing 'Perfect' that echoed across the manicured lawns.

Susan and Martin sat eight rows from, as Susan put it, 'where all the action was taking place'. Hanna reached the summer house where her future husband, the best man and the vicar stood waiting for her. The guests took their seats.

Susan could not help whispering in Martin's ear, "Ah, that's such a lovely song. I bet she was thrilled that Howard picked a really romantic one. Did you know that Ed Sheeran wrote it for his wife-to-be?"

"No, but I do know that it was Hanna who picked the song. Howard wanted the overture from Coppelia by Delibes. His dad wanted Bach's Toccata in E Minor. The bride's parents wanted Frank Sinatra, 'The Best is Yet to Come.' The beauty of families fighting make you want to avoid weddings at all costs."

"Come on, we all need to get married, spend the rest of our life with our soul mate. It must be so wonderful to walk down the aisle dressed in white, the start of a lifelong journey with the person you love."

"It is not the spending the rest of my life with someone that scares me, it is the wedding. If you think that agreeing the choice of song was bad enough, wait until I tell you about the venue choices, dress choices, flower choices, menu choices. I could go on but let's be polite and not spoil their day by yakking. I feel sure there will be more conflict before the end of the day."

Howard and Hanna exchanged their vows, Neville managed to have the ring to hand when required and the newlyweds walked back up the lawned walkway, smiling at their guests as they went. Being kind to the happy couple, the weather provided a steady stream of warm sunshine that only occasionally slipped behind some light fluffy clouds, no doubt taking a breather before once again shining down on the guests.

It was now that time of hanging around while photographs were taken. The immediate family and other relatives were called forward in a set order to record the day in groups of various combinations. Being unrelated guests, Susan and Martin waited patiently for the large group photograph when they would, with any luck, be just about visible somewhere near the back.

As they waited, Susan slipped her arm into Martin's. "It must be nice to be the bride, centre of attention, wearing a fairy tale wedding dress. You know I can't wait to get married. I'm sure it must be wonderful being alongside the man of your dreams for the rest of your life."

"The problem with being married is things go wrong and when they do, it takes legal experts and heaps of money to extract yourself from it. Take the barmaid who works here, the older one with the odd-looking lips, Imogen. She thinks her husband is having an affair and they have been married, she tells me, almost thirty years. Marriage is a time-bomb waiting to go off, best case scenario you die before it explodes."

Susan let go of his arm and asked, "How come you know so much about the barmaid?"

Now this was going to be awkward, of that Martin was sure. Susan knew full well that he had over several years developed a fool proof system of avoiding work and helping people only if it was essential and unavoidable. Hence if he told her he had taken on detecting work following the husband, Susan would at once be aware there was a self-centred reason for him being so generous with his time. The danger was by telling Susan the truth, there was a high probability that she would tell Becky who would in turn tell Mother. It was a quandary which Martin had little hope of avoiding. He told Susan the whole truth.

"You cheeky boy, it's true you would do anything to avoid being sociable with your mother. I'll keep quiet only if you let me come along."

"There's no need Susan, I think even I can manage to follow an old bloke around a couple of pubs."

"That might be so, but I equally don't want to have dinner with Mother, and I can't let you drink alone in a pub; it just wouldn't be right. What time do we pick up the tail?"

He reluctantly nodded in agreement. "You can be so American at times." In return, he got a warm and pleasant hug from Susan.

***

"I thought it would have been a posh sit-down meal. I wasn't expecting to have to walk around this dull room with a plate and a weeny cheese and pickle sandwich."

Susan was not exactly complaining, the buffet table consisted of a great deal more than just the weeny cheese sandwich she had on her plate. There was a wide selection of sandwiches suitable for all dietary requirements as well as some chicken satay sticks, small salmon blinis, vol-au-vents with various fillings, there was a good selection. It was just her expectations were a lot higher than what was currently on offer.

Martin explained that like her, the Phillips family had been in favour of a lavish sit-down meal. Henry Phillips with his chain of butchers had plenty of contacts in the catering trade and the hotel was more than happy to let him source the food. But Hanna's parents were not so excited to have a sit-down meal, for them it was far too formal. They wanted a casual wedding reception with the guests mingling freely, well, that was what they told everyone. The truth Martin had heard was Hanna's mother did not want to spend the entire meal sitting next to Mr Phillips listening to his tedious stories. Following a lot of negotiations and tempers being held in check, a smorgasbord of culinary delights that could be eaten with fingers was agreed by all.

"It makes living together without all the formalities seem very attractive," Susan concluded as she bit into a soggy vegetable samosa.

"It is the controlling families behind the happy couple that create the issues," Martin pointed out before consuming the last of his chicken satay.

They moved towards the sizeable fireplace in one corner of the substantial room, which had originally been designed by Mr Sayers as a ballroom. Hanging from the ceiling were three large crystal chandeliers, flamboyant and opulent, candle-lit back in the day, now converted to electric. The mantelpiece over the fireplace was equally luxurious and it was where Martin had placed his glass of champagne to make eating and plate-holding far easier. He would have much preferred to be sitting down with a knife and fork, yet he did sympathise with Hanna's mother after he had spent last night sitting beside Henry Phillips.

"You must be the gumshoe?"

The question had come from the thin lips of an elderly woman much shorter than both Susan and Martin, who had somehow materialised beside them. She forced her hand into Martin's.

"I'm Vera, Howard's side of this occasion, vaguely related by way of his mother. I won't bore you with the facts, pointless really, after today we might never meet again, unless you and I have a passionate affair upstairs and start a relationship. I've never screwed a gumshoe, so you could be my first. But you look so happy with your partner, who I hear is Susan. Pleased to meet you Susan." Vera now propelled her hand towards Susan who shook hands limply with the lady as she took in her odd features.

Vera was in her late sixties and didn't care about what she wore. Her mismatched clothing colour scheme was testament to that. Red woollen boots, blue paisley jogging bottoms, that highlighted her large behind. Her red t-shirt tucked in and belted showed her middle-aged spread. Her hair was dyed to match her boots, vivid red. Vera had no concern what others thought of her, which was the reason Henry had at first hoped she would not be invited. Having walked out on her husband after thirty years of marriage, assured that their children were in happy secure relationships, she was now proud to be called an environmental activist, chaining herself to railings, glueing herself to trains and generally causing a nuisance in the name of protecting the planet.

"Odd term, don't you think, gumshoe. From 'to gumshoe' which means to sneak around quietly as if wearing gumshoes either to rob, or conversely, to catch thieves. The connotation of gumshoe as a private detective comes from the idea that rubber-soled shoes give the wearer the ability to walk stealthily. I see you're wearing sensible brogues; you must be off duty." Her laugh was almost a cackle. "Always fancied myself as a murder detective," she continued without so much as a breath. "Have you investigated any homicides?"

"No," Susan answered for Martin. "He has, however, murdered a few good margaritas in his time." There was polite laughter between them all.

"My dream is to be offered the chance to review one of those cold cases from years ago. Not that it will ever happen, but we all need dreams. I dream of a world where humans live in harmony with each other and are in accord with nature. That is the dream I am fighting for.

"Good to meet you both, bye for now. I'll leave you two love birds alone and sneak into the garden to have a spliff. Don't think the posh side of the family would approve of me getting high in such prestigious surroundings. I'm happy for you both to join me if you wish, I have plenty. In fact, you both look like the type who might enjoy the odd spliff. If you need anything, here's a local dealer, good prices." She slipped a small grey card into Martin's hand, needlessly stroking his fingers. The scruffy card read: 'BPB' followed by a mobile number.

Having thanked her politely for the information, they both refused the offer of joining a pensioner in the garden to smoke cannabis. Susan and Martin moved away from the fireplace and ended up in the middle of the room.

"She was well weird," Susan commented, as she dropped a dollop of crème fraiche from her salmon blini onto the floor. She walked away from the mess with an innocent expression. Martin followed her, trying not to look guilty. "Do you think she is a sales rep for a local drug gang?"

"I wouldn't like to say. I can tell you that Howard, apart from being a little mean, is a good bloke, it's just his family are a little on the eccentric side. I'd heard of Aunt Vera before, apparently, she once turned up at a christening insisting that they anoint the child with red wine for some bizarre reason. I bet they tried their best to keep her away from the wedding, clearly, they failed."

"Howard is tight-fisted; how do you mean?"

"He only married Hanna because she is short, and therefore needs to buy less material for her wedding dress." Martin smiled and Susan playfully punched him on the arm.

A passing waitress filled their glasses and then moved swiftly onto the next guest. A moment later Mr Henry Phillips and his wife ambushed them. Henry began politely, as if he was the host of the soiree, which in a way he was. Graciously they all agreed the wedding was a sombre yet romantic affair. The weather had been kind and the bride looked stunning. The conversation was no more than the normal banal polite interaction that occurs at any family social event, where half the group hates the other half. You want to tell the truth about others in the room but in the end, you just smile and use trivial words. It was Susan who changed the subject from the wedding.

"Martin tells me that you are a prominent member of the Grantham District Community," Susan stated.

Henry smiled, he adored flattery in any shape or form.

"Well yes, I do hold a certain standing. Many years owning and running a highly successful chain of butchers, Phillips Fillets became synonymous with success."

"Then do you know much about a Roman church on Branston Street? And I am not talking Roman Catholic, I am talking Roman Empire."

"Know them well, or at least their chosen leader, Dave Harvey. Bit of a scallywag as far as business goes. He's the type of guy who likes a quick easy buck. He was one of the first to start selling fireworks from a portacabin in November, the same location as he sells Easter eggs at Easter and flowers on Mother's Day.

"At one time he was running a launderette. Early off the starting blocks with his e-cigarette shop before buying up a cheap church and converting it to his own personal beliefs, if he had any, to become a fully-fledged Roman emperor or whatever he calls himself. He then turned the launderette into a shop selling Roman antiques and replicas. Not the sort of fellow you can easily trust, but us business types need to be on at least speaking terms. He's well known around the shady parts of Grantham. He proclaims now that he has turned over a new leaf having found his true beliefs, no one believes him. Why do you ask?"

"His neighbour maintains that the church prayed over his house and it burnt down."

"Ah, that would be loopy Rodney Watson, not the sharpest knife in the draw. Adequate bus driver but lives his life in a fantasy. Rumour has it he is connected to selling drugs of some sort, but nothing has ever been proven. I also heard he put on his insurance claim form: 'building destroyed by an act of God, a.k.a. Jupiter. Well, I ask you, apart from giving us all a laugh, would any insurance company take such a thing seriously, I doubt it.

"The local rumour mill works overtime for that church about what happens in there, wife swapping, depraved goings on, even human sacrifices. All I would say is that whatever it does get up to, Dave Harvey is somewhere, somehow, making a few pounds for himself. As investigators asking about Dave, I won't pry but I hope you get him."

"Well not so much an investigation," Susan started and stopped as Martin wiped a smear of crème fraiche from her lips. "Thanks. Rodney seems to think he has been hard done by so no harm in us asking a few questions. Can't say more than that," she smiled.

"Are you investigating Dave Harvey?" Mrs Phillips spoke for the first time; her question was genuine, and

Susan picked up a slight tone of tension. She was dressed to impress, as the mother of the groom that was her duty, a role she took very seriously.

"Not really, let's face it I doubt it was an act of God that burnt Rodney's house down. But we think it's worth asking a couple of questions all the same."

"About his church, now that makes sense," this time Mrs Phillips tone appeared to be more relaxed.

The change made Susan think. It was either a woman's instinct or the champagne, but whichever it was, she said, "Yet his church shop is still an interesting side line of the inquiry, connections come in all shapes and sizes. Keep altering the shop from one use to another, lots of paperwork and stuff, always a little suspicious." At this point Susan was not exactly sure what she was saying, she was, to coin a phrase, rabbiting on about nothing. She was just talking as if she was throwing a wide selection of bait into a river to see what she could catch. Susan thought that any entrepreneur who kept swapping business interests is normally on the fiddle with taxation, pushing the regulations to the limit. She had read something about that when she had been faced with a mound of paperwork to become a director of Hayden Investigations.

"I'm sure Mr Harvey had all the correct planning permissions for change of use," Mrs Phillips pointed out. Something that Susan had not expected to hear or even considered; it was a curious answer.

Henry interrupted; the conversation was not moving in a direction that he appeared comfortable with. "If you're interested in the fire at Rodney's place, I'll introduce you to a man who knows a lot more. The insurance broker handling the claim is in the chamber with me and a good friend. Maybe together you can come up with something. He's here today, I'll get him to have a word with you."

At that point Henry decided that he had to speak to a man he had vaguely pointed at. Thanked them courteously and walked off, his wife followed obediently behind.

"That was an odd conversation, didn't you think so, Martin? His wife seemed a little on edge and Henry was happy to change the subject back to the fire."

"Her son has just got married; I think all mothers are a little edgy on a day like this."

***

Her third glass of bubbly resulted in Susan handing her glass to Martin and declaring that she needed to find the ladies, leaving him standing alone amongst the guests holding two glasses. He was not alone for long.

"You look like a naughty boy," the voice came from behind him. It no doubt came from the woman who arrived at his side after having playfully slapped his bottom.

"Two glasses...naughty, naughty."

She was as tall as Martin, maybe in her late fifties, dressed in an expensive-looking outfit, pink printed flowers on a rose material, matching shoes and handbag, both a deeper pink than her dress. In her blonde hair, she wore a pink fascinator which sat at an unusual angle on her head, with its fine feathers again in a shade of pink. Martin watched as she swayed gently on her high heels.

"I've just had the one glass...honest. Just too many times refilled. So I am, I'll confess to you, you naughty boy, I'm a little squiffy. Can you tell?"

Martin smiled, her speech appeared to be a little slurred and she was unsteady on her feet. He gave her the benefit of the doubt, not that he had one. "No, I wouldn't have guessed."

"Good. I'm the blide's mother, can't let her side down. Are you one of Howard's buddies?"

"Yes, the same rugby club. Lovely ceremony, I thought."

She leaned in close; Martin could feel her warm alcohol-infused breath on his cheek and her hand on his bottom.

"Cost an absolute fortune so old Henry, him with the lamb chops and saus..saus..sauag... bangers, can impress all his poshie friends. The kids wanted a quickie. Oops," she brought her hand up to her mouth, before clarifying, "not a quickie-quickie, a quick wedding. Do I sound a little tipsy? And cheap, no not me, a cheap wedding. Dear me, I haven't drunk more than two glasses of sherry for years now. The only downside is the family, the Phillips are a rum lot, all that stuff in the papers. Still my sweet daughter says she's in love. Good luck to them that's what I say. At least the son seems a better deal than the randy old man. Oops, I mean between you and me, you being on their side of the fence."

"Don't you like old man Phillips?" Martin asked, wondering what was at the back of her addled mind.

"That stuff about the launderette last year; you must have read about it. At least the son isn't a butcher. Butchers are a rum lot, don't you think? Oh, look there's Hanna's aunt, or to be more formal, my sister, nice talking to you."

Before Martin could ask any further questions about the launderette, the bride's mother swayed off towards a small group of younger women, leaving him a little puzzled. That was twice within the last hour a launderette had been mentioned. He was surprised such things still existed, let alone came up in conversations at a wedding.

Susan soon replaced the bride's mother at Martin's side. Having seen the interaction, she commented that she could not leave him alone for a second without old women throwing themselves at him. She also helpfully pointed out that any wife he might take on would need to spend most of her time fighting off the opposition.

"Then I'd best keep my eyes open for a wife who is also a warrior queen. Plus," he added, "a person who can hold her drink. Hanna's mother clearly cannot handle more than the odd glass here or there without saying the strangest of things. She mentioned a launderette, but she was connecting it to old man Phillips."

"I'm beginning to think that Grantham suffers from a lot of inbreeding, what with the old drug lady dealer, mysterious goings on around a launderette and I'm sure I've just seen an old man sitting down over there eating sandwiches out of a plastic lunch box. I think he might have brought his own food to the wedding."

"Ah, that sounds like Edwin Stewart."

***

Edwin was sitting on a red velvet chair hunched over a clear plastic lunch box to avoid crumbs from his ham and pickle sandwich spilling onto the floor, he liked to be orderly. He was pleased to accept the invitation from his godson. Everyone accepted that he would be bringing his own food, which today apart from the sandwich also included a Penguin Bar and a banana. Although he was happy to let the other guests consume the wedding buffet, he did join them in the consumption of champagne, his only vice. Even at home he would order a case of champagne each week from the local supermarket who delivered it along with his frozen ready meals and other essential groceries. Though he might have gathered odd comments from the delivery drivers, for him champagne and one-person ready meals were an essential part of life. There was something about drinking champagne that gave him a euphoric feeling of being young again. The alcohol might be harming his liver, but his mind was as sharp as it had ever been.

As Martin and Susan walked towards him, Martin explained the oddities of the man still wearing the Homburg hat with a large feather in its band. Welcoming the young couple and remaining firmly seated with his lunch on his lap, Edwin hoped that Susan's problem was fully sorted out last night and that Martin had done his bit. The ambiguity of his words was not lost on Susan.

"I'm glad we've met up again," Martin began. "This morning I picked up what I think is a small coin, it could be Roman, so I wondered if you as the coin expert could give me your opinion of it. It's in my room, it wouldn't take me long to fetch it."

"Pointless young man, my eyes are not what they were, I need a rather strong magnifying glass to examine any sort of coin nowadays. If it is a Roman coin, even more so, small little buggers. You are more than welcome to pop around to my home in the morning, bring it with you and I'll give it the once over. Where did you find it?"

"In the garden of a burnt-out house close to the Roman Empire Church."

"Ah, that would explain it. You did not look to me like the kind of chap to go around digging up muddy fields in the hope of finding treasure. It could be one of Mr Harvey's stock which he sells successfully around the globe. I missed out on the internet, wrong generation, but I do a bit of surfing on the web and he seems to be doing well with his business. You must come as well, young lady."

"Sorry," Susan apologised, "I have a spa treatment session booked. Taking advantage of the hotel facilities to indulge myself."

"Such a pity, maybe another time."

A squeaky voice spoke from behind Martin, "Mr Hayden? Sorry to interrupt, Mr Phillips said you wanted a word."

Both Susan and Martin turned to see a short man with a mouse-like face in part hidden by sunglasses that were slowly lightening. He held a full glass of champagne and wore a shiny suit, shiny through wear not fashion Susan thought. His tie looked to represent a military regiment; it lay on a plain white shirt.

"I'm Patrick Bastard and before you ask, my surname is French, it's not a description of my birth right. You were asking about Rodney and his fire?"

Patrick was most forthcoming about the facts surrounding the fire. As the local insurance broker, he had handled the claim and knew all there was to know about the incident. There might be rules over data protection and client confidentiality, which were disregarded as a favour to Mr Phillips and as Patrick pointed out, 'Rodney is not the discreet type in the first place, having told the local newspaper about the fire and the cause.'

The fire began in the living room, close to a place where Rodney kept flowers and photographs of his deceased mother, in a sort of hallowed shrine. It was not exactly clear how the fire had ignited, although there were small traces of an accelerant which might have been no more than a small amount of nail polish or a cup full of turpentine. It had been generally accepted by the insurance company that it might well have started accidentally, but Rodney was not admitting to anything. It could be proved without doubt that Rodney was out of the house at the time driving a bus. In fact, Patrick confirmed that they were about to start asking for estimates to restore the house when Rodney suggested what had happened,

"He told us it was a Roman deity that had caused the fire in revenge for him leaving that group of miscreants in the church next door to him. They apparently started the fire through their prayers. Well, I have heard some pretty outlandish explanations in my time, but that one ranked in the top three.

"For the insurance company and I as the broker, it was back to the drawing board. If he said it was a god, who were we to argue. The thing is because he changed his mind, the insurance company began to suspect foul play, a deliberate act to start the fire. Any excuse for them not to pay out."

"So you investigated the church?" Susan asked, noting that Patrick's glasses had now cleared completely to reveal a narrow pair of grey-green eyes.

"We did ask questions, but they were not going to admit to anything and there's no proof. We're in a state of flux. We're not too keen on paying out as we do suspect foul play somewhere along the line. Plus, Rodney doesn't seem too bothered about hurrying the process. Odd situation, I'm sure you will agree."

As the mouse-like Patrick Bastard left the couple to mingle with other guests, Susan's only comment was, "Odd situations do seem to be the norm around these parts."

Chapter 6

"I thought the wedding was highly successful, eminently enjoyable, let's hope their marriage goes as well," Edwin stated as he turned the small coin between his fingers. With the help of a powerful lamp and an equally effective magnifying glass, Edwin looked for clues that would help him to further identify the coin which appeared to be at first glance a silver denarius.

As instructed, Martin had arrived just after ten in the morning with the coin. As tempted as he was, Martin declined the offer of a glass of champagne and accepted a glass of water instead. The home was cluttered as he had expected. The one-bedroom bungalow was located on the edge of a large field, which at the present time was a dazzling shade of yellow from the ripening rape. Even though Martin had commented favourably on the view from Edwin's living room, the old man poo-pooed it, complaining that the pollen from the field gave him headaches and bouts of blocked sinuses.

Although the room was strewn with books, magazines and newspapers, there was a kind of vague order to it. The books were neatly stacked on the floor in piles of the same height. The height was exactly reproduced in the heaps of mostly trade magazines and newspapers that were scattered around. One wall was filled with a mix of bookshelves with many hardbacks and wall-mounted glass cabinets displaying coins and bank notes from around the world.

Edwin put the magnifier down, turned off the light, took a small gulp from his champagne and then moved towards the racks of books. He located a particularly large well-thumbed paperback, flicked it open, turned a few pages then appeared to read the text, all in silence. Martin felt as if he was awaiting a life-or-death diagnosis from a surgeon.

With respectful care, Edwin replaced the book to its rightful place amongst the other tomes and returned to his chair and his champagne, which he sipped once again.

"Well," he concluded, "your little coin does appear to be Roman. Minted in the era of Emperor Hadrian, a denarius coin back in the day was worth about the same as a twenty-pound note. Funny chap Hadrian, born in Spain to an Italian family. Had a difficult childhood, father died when he was only ten and then he was brought up by his second cousin. Anyway, I am sure you have heard of Hadrian and his wall to keep the Scots out. Lots of other achievements as well, not that I am an expert on Roman history, coins are my thing.

"As I was saying this appears to be a denarius of Emperor Hadrian, in post from 117 to 138 AD. This particular coin may have been minted around 132AD, towards the end of Hadrian's rule. You see on the back, Roma, a female Roman deity."

Edwin leaned forward and pointed out the figure to Martin, then turned it over and pointed out the head of Emperor Hadrian. Leaving the coin in Martin's hand, Edwin leaned back in his chair and took a large swallow from his glass.

"Not bad condition considering it could be almost two thousand years old, which you would think would make it worth more than the hundred pounds I estimate it to be worth if you sold it at auction."

"You say could be, it is a real Roman coin?" Martin asked, wondering about Edwin's choice of words.

"That is the bigger question. It appears to be genuine, but that is not to say it is."

"But it could be a fake?"

"Let me explain a little more about coins from antiquity."

There came a point as Edwin was explaining the fundamentals of coins that Martin felt he should be taking notes to be sure he had not missed anything.

Edwin, with the proficiency of a certain history teacher Martin recalled from his boarding school, explained that Roman coins could be faked in modern times as well as during the lifetime of the Roman Empire. Often populations that had been conquered by the Romans, decided to make copies of the currency the vanquishers inflicted on them.

The silver denarius was a common target to be faked. During those times, silver was worth about a hundred times more than copper, so a copper disc could be covered with a very thin film of silver, then striking it with false dies to match a denarius giving the impression the coin was silver, handing the counterfeiters a handsome profit margin.

The whole situation was not helped by the Romans themselves, Edwin pointed out.

The denarius was originally made of almost pure silver. Various emperors lessened its weight, as Trajan, Hadrian's second cousin who brought him up did, to pay for public works as well as expensive wars. Trajan added copper to dilute the silver content. By the end of the second century, the silver content had been reduced to less than a half.

"The upshot of all this," Edwin concluded, "is that Roman coins come in various categories. You have the original coins that were minted legitimately by the Republic. You also have those which were minted by local criminals from conquered countries during the same period, making them just as collectable. None of these coins are really consistent in their weight or composition, therefore making a judgement as to where your coin fits into the history is a lot harder than you might think. Then you must add into that mix modern day forgeries, which take advantage of the less than standard denarius."

"Can you make an educated guess?"

Edwin stroked the underside of his chin thoughtfully before he spoke with a wry smile.

"My educated guess is based on my personal theories. First, where did you find it? Next to the Temple of Jupiter in Grantham. That temple, or more correctly Mr Harvey, sells such coins on their website and in his shop. He has glowing reviews from his online customers, appearing to do a very good trade through the internet. His shop, as you would expect, does not have much footfall, Roman coin collectors in Grantham and its environs are not thick on the ground."

"You're saying it's genuine?"

"I haven't finished my theories yet. On the face of it, considering what I have said, you would expect it to be from the Roman Republic. But, as an ex-coin dealer, there is one thing that both mystifies me and troubles me.

"It concerns me that Mr Harvey was at one time, rumour has it, operating a brothel from the flat above his launderette, although nothing was proven. But it does show me he is not above breaking the law. He also seems to have the ability to have a very high stock level. In my day, I used to have to scrabble around to obtain a very modest amount of such items whereas he seems to have no trouble obtaining a plentiful supply. Maybe identifying his source might lend itself to proving or disproving the authenticity of the coin you hold in your hand."

Martin rolled the coin between his fingers, nothing seemed to be conclusive about the small disc with the head of Hadrian on it. Yet any thoughts that he had about the coin were washed away at the mention of a launderette and a brothel. Hadn't he been told about a launderette yesterday at the wedding by the bride's mother? Supposedly it was in the papers and connected to the Phillips family. Now, according to Edwin, it is this Mr Harvey, the leader of the Roman Church, that is connected to some bad press around a launderette.

"I thought that story was connected to Mr Phillips?" Martin cast the question in the same way he might cast a fly when trout fishing, not that he would ever want to stand in the middle of a cold river throwing fake flies into the water.

"I'm surprised that as you are new to the area, you have even heard of the story, let alone any connection to old man Phillips. What have you heard?"

"Not a lot, just that Henry Phillips was connected to a derogatory story, I gather connected to a launderette."

Edwin refilled his glass carefully to ensure the bubbles did not fizz up and overflow.

"Ah, well in a way Henry was connected to the property. Technically, as I understand it, he was renting the flat above the launderette, but then denied having anything to do with the brothel that the police uncovered. The two young ladies living there were adamant that they were totally independent. In a town like Grantham, gossip is rife, but nothing has been proven. Can I suggest that you speak to Henry Phillips yourself, I am sure he can offer an explanation. I just think Dave Harvey is a very shady person."

***

"How was the spa?" Martin asked, as he drove away from the hotel towards Dave Harvey's house on the affluent side of Grantham. Not that he had ever imagined that Grantham had an affluent side. He classified the town as one of those small insignificant market towns, that existed by a quirk of history and usually went to sleep by seven in the evening. The most exciting event he could imagine happening was a meeting of purple-haired old ladies discussing the merits of baking a sponge cake and then icing it.

"Oh, I feel so much better. I had one of those Himalayan Salt Treatments. Feel my skin." She offered Martin her bare arm to decide for himself. As Martin stroked her skin, he had to admit it felt good, very good. He did have one question.

"I thought a spa massage was about oils and perfumes, not sprinkling salt over your body."

If Susan was being honest, she had thought the same when she booked the Himalayan Salt Treatment with the receptionist, who was still as grumpy as she had been when they checked in. No doubt she associated Susan with problems, which was a little unfair, if not entirely untrue.

Susan had expected to be sprinkled with salt, that was either rubbed in or brushed off, a bit like an exfoliating scrub she used as a teenager to rid herself of spots.

"Don't be daft, Martin, that would make me a chip. No, they use blocks of salt, which they rub over your body. The blocks are warm as well, so the treatment makes you feel cosy and snug, really good."

"Wouldn't a hot water bottle do the same and be a lot cheaper than what I am guessing you paid?"

"It's more than just that, it works on your Parasympathetic Nervous System."

"Are you sure you have one of those?"

"We all have a Parasympathetic Nervous System, even you. Plus, we have a Sympathetic Nervous System. I'm not sure you are that sympathetic though. Let me explain."

"There's no need for that."

"Yes, there is."

She did explain, repeating most of what the therapist had told her about the treatment, describing how the heat activates the Parasympathetic Nervous System. She also pointed out the human nervous system can be broken down into two parts: the Sympathetic and the Parasympathetic Nervous Systems, which are the two different roads that your nerve impulses can take. The Sympathetic Nervous System is the "fight or flight" response.

"The Parasympathetic Nervous System is the resting response. Years ago, when we lived in caves, our Sympathetic Nervous System was used to protect us from dangers, such as running from a bear. Nowadays, our Sympathetic Nervous System is activated by stress from the fast-paced society we live in. When we are feeling stressed out, our Sympathetic Nervous System is activated. The same mechanism that was used to protect people from bears is now being activated almost constantly, making it hard for people to rest and relax."

"Since when did you find it hard to rest and relax?"

"I'll have you know I can hide my true feelings extremely well. I think you are jealous and impressed at just how educational a beauty treatment can be. Plus, I am now full of positive energy."

That was all Martin needed, a Susan high on positive energy. Such a state would run the risk of her asking the wrong questions at the wrong time and landing him in a mess.

***

The house looked the same as any one of the other six large, detached houses that populated Bryan Close. The cul-de-sac, on the outskirts of Grantham, was equally prestigious and pretentious. The large neat square patch of overly green grass ran alongside the driveway that was congested with two sizeable Mercedes cars, each with a personalised number plate. Such things seemed to be essential if you wished to park in Bryan Close.

The large double garage to the right of the house could easily have accommodated both cars, but for the fact that in this cul-de-sac showing off your wealth was the rule.

When Dave Harvey moved into the close to occupy the six-bedroom house once owned by a well-respected captain of industry, residents were unsure what to expect. They had heard rumours and troubling stories about Dave and his business affairs, activities that did not readily fit with the modus operandi of the other locals, although a small number were more than happy to doctor their tax returns and still denounce alleged criminals like Dave Harvey. However, the arrival of his two new Mercedes with their respective registration plates, had gone a long way to dispel the fears of most of the neighbours.

From what Martin had heard of Dave Harvey's exploits, he was inclined to support the general viewpoint of the residents. Yet the way Dave Harvey, following a simple phone call, had happily offered to see them, then warmly invited them into his home, surprised Martin and made him reconsider his rushed opinion. Dave ushered the two strangers into a large living room and politely asked what he could do to help.

It was not that he was a kind and generous person, in fact far from it, it was just he did not like to be seen talking to strangers on his doorstep. The snooping, interfering neighbours would suspect that the police were trying to gain entry to question him. Many still suspected, correctly, that he was a shady individual.

While Susan explained the purpose of their visit, which in Martin's opinion was pointless, he gazed around the room. Part of him had expected an eccentric house full of Roman artifacts. He had fully anticipated walking into a home that reflected the taste and decor of Rome under Julius Caesar, together with an unconventional man walking around the house in a toga.

In fact, the room was sleek and modern, nothing appeared to be out of place. A large corner unit provided the seating which dominated the room, with a wall-mounted large screen television coming a close second. Arguably the rectangular marble coffee table might have been found in a Roman villa, but it would not have had sleek design lines in the same way as the one Martin was examining. On the coffee table lay a paperback: 'The Trials of Loreli', by Mike Chandler. Martin had never heard of the book.

"You're telling me things I'm already aware of," Dave began to respond to Susan, largely ignoring Martin. "Rodney has for some time now held a grudge against our beliefs. I should mention he was at one time fully supportive and his contribution to our worship was valued.

If I had to point to the reason things turned sour, it would be our strong belief that left-handed people bring bad luck. Not that we were going to cast him out, but he seemed to take it personally. He can often be moody.

"It was around that time when his girlfriend walked out on him, which upset him terribly, he at once blamed us for the breakdown of their relationship. He said we had cursed him for being left-handed and it was our way of getting rid of him, which could not be further from the truth. Even so, soon after that he stopped attending services and never spoke another civil word to any of us."

"What exactly do you do in the church?" Susan asked, realising this man was talking about worship and services. She knew it had to be far removed from any branch of the Church of England.

"We are part of a global network of likeminded people who wish to follow the moral code of the Romans. The overarching network is called Nova Roma. My group is part of a subgroup, The House of Jupiter, Grantham branch. I am the Senior Senator of the followers.

"We wish to promote the restoration of the classical Roman religion, culture, virtues and shared Roman ideals. For us being Roman is more than just worshiping the gods, it's a way of life. I now have over one hundred who regularly attend my Temple of Jupiter."

"Why would you want to follow an empire that disappeared hundreds of years ago?" Susan asked, not fully understanding his explanation.

"You are missing the point young lady, we admire and respect the Roman way of life, their values, many of which have been lost in these modern times."

"Yeah, slaves are something we all miss," Martin added with more than a hint of contempt. "As for gladiators, well, nothing like a good bit of blood and gore to make a perfect Saturday afternoon, is there?"

"Slavery was not new back then; in the same way it did not die when the influence of the Roman Empire waned. Humans have a very bad habit of inflicting pain on those deemed not to be worthy. The great freedom loving democracy of the United States has its foundations built on the genocide of the indigenous population, followed by the structured bulk import of slaves to ensure that America became a great trading nation on the back of very cheap labour. That is just one example, there are countless others.

"A modern-day version of the Roman Empire, the Roman Republic Cultural Group, which is an international organisation, is an excellent example of amending Roman life to fit with modern values. They would be the first to acknowledge that exact restoration is not always possible or desirable. We offer an opportunity for disillusioned people to try an alternative lifestyle, rather than that laid down by governed or traditional religions."

It is often the case, that the first time you meet someone you have a predetermined idea of what they might be like. Martin, having spoken to Henry Phillips, had expected Dave Harvey would be very rough round the edges. A man who would not shy away from getting into a brawl, a virtual villain and by Martin's standards, a man not too well-educated. The Mr Harvey who now sat close to him did not appear to operate at the low-level he had thought he might. Dave Harvey appeared to be well-schooled, knowledgeable, precise in his words and the sort of chap Martin might have invited around for dinner.

"Maybe the two of you should come along to one of our festivals. We are having one later today, it's our dies natalis, our founding day, the group is two years old. There will be lots of members there and you'll get the chance to ask them about Rodney. I think you will find that he is a little unstable and living in a fantasy world."

Susan wanted to say, *'And you are living in what?'* Sensibly for Susan, she pushed that question to one side and asked another.

"Rodney also told us that you wanted to buy his house to expand your church, is that true?"

"Yes, in part," Dave smiled, "we are looking to expand our temple complex. Our dream is to have a smaller replica of the Temple of Jupiter that was destroyed in Pompeii back in 79AD. Rodney's house sits in a large parcel of land. We asked him if he would be amicable to selling us a strip of land that's at the back of his house and largely left untouched by his mother before her death and ever since. He was at first considering it, yet after the falling out, he refused. His accusation that Jupiter burnt his house down and implicating us, is totally incorrect. We were never interested in the house, and even if we were, burning it down would be a bit like cutting off our nose to spite our face."

Susan was still sceptical about Dave considering what she had heard about this man. It was time for, in her own words, a Jim Rockford moment.

"I have heard you have had a number of business interests in the last few years, including a launderette with a massage parlour above it. Women offering a special hands-on service, that sounds a little shady to me."

Dave stood up and walked towards the large television screen, then turned around to face his accusers. He was in his forties, not well-built, average height, if there is such a thing, but strong enough and brave enough to not step away from a fight. His face shape, very much a square, was adorned by neat hair and a beard. He liked to think he was the spitting image of Hadrian; he even had his hair permed to reinforce the illusion. The beard he grew was a little too grey for him, so he dyed it jet black. It was more the long Roman nose that was the winning factor in his quest to look Roman.

"You told me you are both up here for a wedding, just popping into the area for the weekend. You find a dog, take the word of the owner at face value and then, I imagine, listen to some locals who were at the wedding. From this, you deduce that I am a villain, just as so many people do. They are all wrong.

"I am an entrepreneur who takes advantage of the ever-changing market to make money. I take risks, some fail, some succeed. Fortunately for me most have succeeded, hence this large house and equally large bank balance. There are others who are jealous, nothing more, nothing less, they are jealous of my success. They are the ones who start nasty rumours questioning how I make so much money unless I am a criminal.

"It's true that I did have a launderette with a flat above it which I rented out, why wouldn't I? The fact is the occupants decided to run a brothel to make extra money. I only found out when I closed the launderette to open my Roman replica shop. I now have new tenants for the flat who are not pimps."

"Didn't you report them to the police?" Susan asked.

"I would have but the tenant asked me not to. Which, before you ask, is not a simple open and shut case. The renter was Henry Phillips, who you clearly know, he pointed out that the two girls in the flat were the ones responsible for, how shall I say, providing the service which they did on their own initiative. Given his reputation in the town, I would've needed concrete evidence if I went to the police. His word against mine; you can imagine whose side the police would take. He gave up the tenancy and left. The whole thing was brushed away and in the main forgotten.

"People are always quick to judge me and my church. I do not have a criminal record; I don't break laws and I really would like you to attend our dies natalis to see for yourselves. Then you can judge me and my followers, not just listen to the words of others."

"Where do you source your coins from?" The question Martin posed surprised both Dave and Susan.

"Various places. Not that I would share the exact details of where my coins come from with you, that's what they describe as being commercially sensitive."

"It surprises me that there are so many Roman coins available, given your shop has stock and your online business seems to have a great deal of coins for sale." Martin wondered if Dave would take the bait, rise to his allegation. Not that he was exactly sure what he was trying to accuse Dave of. Edwin's comments had been vague, and the old man did not want to expand further. Even so, Martin believed he was trying to suggest Dave was making modern fakes.

"You might or might not know that as well as authentic Roman coins, there are also counterfeit coins from the same era, which are just as sought after. Most of them can be located in archaeological digs in Eastern Europe. I have good contacts and hence have a very resilient supply chain."

***

As Martin drove away, there was a distinct difference of opinion in the car.

"You have to admit Susan, he does seem a nice bloke. He spoke well, seemed calm and friendly, well educated. I just cannot equate what we have heard about him with the man we have just met. If anything, it just strengthens my opinion that Rodney is a troublemaker and, on the whole, not very nice."

"That's because you associate money with honesty and being a good chappie. You also associate common people with being poor, having rubbish jobs and generally being dishonest. It's what we call in the trade, being a snob."

"You know full well I'm not a snob."

"I think you'll find you're still a bit of an elitist. Answer me this, Dave's house, what did you make of it?"

"Is this going to be one of your trick questions?"

"No, just tell me what you thought of it."

Martin negotiated a roundabout, narrowly avoiding a motorcycle before he answered, "It was a nice place, neat, tidy, well decorated, not over the top. I would say it was very sophisticated."

"Exactly," Susan exclaimed, as if Martin had just admitted to some terrible crime. "There was not one example or hint of him being a Roman culture fanatic. I would have thought that anyone who was into Roman stuff would have a load of weird junk around them to keep the Roman mood going. Nothing. And the other thing..."

"There is an additional thing?"

"Yes, who goes from having a launderette to heading up a bunch of oddballs who want to revive Roman culture, in just two years. I'll tell you, someone who does not play by the rules."

"Susan, you are making no sense whatsoever. People change, those in business seek out opportunities to make money."

"Oh, he's making money all right, it's just how legal it all is. I think the chance to chat to the members of his weird congregation will be helpful."

Chapter 7

"Why do old people have to have such a structured routine in their lives?" Becky asked. Her tone of voice sounded gloomy, a mixture of sadness and frustration. It had been a tiring day and it was still only mid-afternoon. She absentmindedly stirred the cocktail that the barmaid had placed in front of her. It was a classic Martini, shaken, not stirred, just the same way James Bond drank them. Colin had bought it for her because of the astonishing fact that she had never had such a drink. Most of the cocktails she had tried in her life were flamboyant concoctions.

An earlier conversation held as Colin was driving Mother and her back to the hotel provided a source of both amusement and education for Becky, especially when Mother joined in. Like most odd conversations the start could not be exactly recalled, it just happened.

Colin admitted that he had trouble believing that Becky had never tried a James Bond Martini, shaken, not stirred. He then asked, had she ever had a 'celebrity drink' in her life. Becky had drunk a wide range of alcoholic drinks, but had never heard of celebrity drinks.

"You must have had a White Russian; I assumed it was compulsory for you young ones. In the film, 'Big Lebowski', Jeff Bridges' character drinks nine White Russians and spills one of them. If I recall correctly, the drink is: two parts vodka, one part Kahlua, one part cream."

"Never heard of it," Becky admitted, before Colin suggested another.

"Alright, easy one this time. Absinthe, have you tried that?"

"That old French drink? Once, thought it was dreadful."

"At least you have tried it, you get two points for that. It was the preferred drink of Pablo Picasso. At least you're now up and running. When we get back, I'll buy you a James Bond Martini."

Then a voice boomed from the backseat of the car, "What about Scotch with canned vegetables?" Mother suggested.

"That's not a drink," Colin pointed out. "That, is an actual travesty of human rights."

"Well, Colleen," Mother was still refusing to call him by his correct name as much as Becky had tried to correct her mistake. She was just not comfortable using a male name to interact with a female clothed person. "That is where you are wrong. It's a known fact that Dirk Bogarde drank Scotch, large amounts, I once heard from a film director who had worked with him. It was when Dirk was filming 'The African Queen', only he and John Houston did not come down with dysentery. They were the only ones in the cast and crew who were not affected. They put it down to the Scotch and canned vegetables that they both lived on. Dirk Bogarde said anytime a fly bit him, it just dropped dead. I loved that man," Mother laughed discreetly.

"Well dearie, I can't promise that the hotel will be prepared to help us on that one. I was thinking more like a Gin Rickey, favoured by F. Scott Fitzgerald. It's made up of gin, clearly, a bit of lime juice and club soda, which is American for sparkling water. Just proves how pretentious the yanks are."

"It sounds like diluted gin to me," Becky suspected, "but worth trying it, I reckon. This Scott guy with the diluted gin, is he the same bloke who found one of the poles? Can't remember if it was north or south."

"My dear Becky," Mother spouted up from the back of the car, "Captain Scott was at the South Pole; F. Scott Fitzgerald was a novelist. You really need to read more; you'll learn so much. I am just thankful you are more astute when it comes to overseeing my accounts."

Colin stirred his Gin Rickey and looked at Becky. Who would have thought that Becky with her long legs, short skirts, blonde hair, tight blouse and make-up, which he judged to be over the top, would endear herself to Martin's mother. Becky did have a certain innocence about her which maybe brought out the mothering instinct in Mrs Hayden, something that Martin had failed to do all his life.

"You're right, old people do like their routines. I presume Mother is upstairs as we speak, adjusting her outfit, touching up her make-up and brushing her hair in preparation for her four o'clock tea with a piece of fruit cake, which will satisfy her until seven-thirty when she sits down to her evening meal. I can only presume," Colin offered his best guess, "that it's a way of ensuring they haven't died and gone to heaven, a place that must have a totally different time zone to us mere mortals stuck on earth. Either that or when you're Mrs Hayden's age, you need to make the most of the time you have left."

Becky nodded her head, then sipped her Martini, which produced a warm smile of approval.

"That's nice, not sure James Bond can fight the baddies after a couple, but yummy all the same. I thought the old dear was going to lose it today; I've never seen her so mad," Becky stated, recalling the events of a frustrating afternoon in her mind.

***

Earlier, the three of them had left soon after lunch which was from twelve-thirty to one-thirty, the time Mother had it each day. The atmosphere in the car was congenial as Colin drove towards the centre of Grantham and then to the grocery shop where Margaret Thatcher was born.

Mother, with an unusual tone of excitement in her voice, recalled the occasion that she had spoken to the then current Prime Minister. That had been the time when she visited the Hayden family business, a manufacturing company making a wide range of screws that were exported all over the world. Mrs Hayden had never felt so proud to be alongside her husband as she was when meeting England's first female Prime Minister, they chatted as if they were old friends. Then they were proud to provide refreshments for the celebrity and her entourage in the hallowed Hayden Board of Directors' Room. They talked about unions, increasing trade with the United States and then, as women do, recipes for the cake that Mrs Thatcher had made for her son on his return from being lost in Africa. It was a recipe that Mother was able to recite to this day and did enlighten both Colin and Becky into the secrets of the Prime Minister's Victoria cake.

"Mrs Thatcher told me her secret was sieving the flour twice, making the sponge incredibly light and airy. I, of course, tried it soon after and as ever the lady was so right. I say if you can make a light Victoria Sponge then you deserve to rule over the country."

Colin wanted to ask if Mother knew if the Queen could make such a light cake, if not perhaps she should abdicate, but he thought better of it. He did not want to spoil the light-hearted mood.

There was another time Mother remembered, a charity event at the Victoria and Albert Museum, when to Mrs Hayden's delight Mrs Thatcher recalled the visit to the screw factory and the discussion over cake. That story was related to friends and family on many occasions, until such time that Mr Hayden, Martin's father, put his foot down and told his wife to put the whole episode behind her.

After the personal stories, Mrs Hayden went on to praise the female leader's ability to do the right thing: putting down the miners, knocking Argentina for six and reducing taxation for those of us who provide employment for the masses. Becky and Colin looked at each other, raised their eyebrows but graciously kept quiet.

Mr Roberts, Maggie's father, had his shop on the corner of North Parade, now a busier crossroads than it had been when Mr Roberts walked his little daughter along the streets. With modern parking restrictions, Colin needed to leave the car a little way away from the famous grocer's shop. It was a pleasantly warm day, so Mother was more than happy to walk the short distance, taking in the atmosphere and adoring the pavements where the great lady spent her childhood. They arrived at the corner where the shop stood, no longer looking as it had back in her day.

"Colleen, are you sure this is the right place?" Mother looked at the shop that now occupied the famous corner, it was no longer a greengrocer.

"Yes, wonder woman was born right here, well, not in the street, up above the shop."

"You have brought me to the wrong place Colleen, she was born on Barrowby Road, this is North Parade. Take me to the correct place at once."

Colin took three steps forward, now standing on the edge of the crossroads and indicated a road sign for the dissecting road.

"Here we go," he pointed at the road name, "Barrowby Road, still the same shop."

Mother stood and looked around, there was an appalled look on her face. Any passer-by might have imagined that the little old lady had just been told she had two hours to live.

"Well, this is an absolute travesty. There is nothing here to indicate to the local population that the great woman herself was born in these humble streets. A strong woman, who dragged herself from this mediocre town and became one of the great leaders of the world. They marked the birthplace of Winston Churchill well enough, why not Mrs Thatcher."

Colin brushed his hair back. The brunette wig he was wearing today was prone to fly-away hair from the breeze that was whipping around the corner. He answered Mother, "Well to be fair, Winston Churchill was born at Blenheim Palace, the clue is in the second word, palace. Your Maggie was born in a small flat above a shop, not the same opulence as the Churchills."

"That is not the point Colleen. There should be something here to mark the historic significance of this site for future generations."

"There's a plaque up there." Becky pointed helpfully to a small handmade one with faded painted letters above the shop front.

Mother and Colin both looked up. Colin refrained from commenting; Mother was not so timid.

"Well, that is a dreadful waste of time. We must do something about this injustice. We must go back to the hotel and devise a plan of action. I will not let this rest until there is adequate and suitable recognition. What is wrong with the people of Grantham, are they ashamed of her good work?"

Becky had heard terrible stories about the injustices that Mrs Thatcher applied to many working-class people. Her grandpappy had not a single good word to say for the Iron Lady. Becky opened her mouth to repeat some of the tirades her grandpappy voiced during the Thatcher years. Fortunately, Colin saw her lips open and his expression told her that she would be better not to say any more and just travel back to the hotel.

***

"What does she expect to do about the Iron Lady's birthplace?" Becky questioned as she finished her Martini.

"Never underestimate the wrath or influence of a little old lady, from an upper-class background, to inflict on others. They know the right people; they have the right words, and they have the time and money to do it."

Colin ordered another Gin Rickey for himself and one for Becky, ensuring she continued along the road of celebrity cocktails without pause. If Mother was going to be in a combative mood for the rest of the evening, both would need a few more drinks to get them through the meal.

Becky gave a murmur of approval as she sampled the Gin Rickey while Colin took the opportunity to ask her a question that had been troubling him. He wished he had asked it at the time, but Mother's tirade had distracted him.

"Becky, after we had parked the car and were walking down North Parade towards the birthplace, did you notice a block of flats?"

"Can't say I did."

"Well, I noticed a man going into one of them, pushing a woman into the doorway, not really in an aggressive way more of an encouraging way. I didn't think much of it then, just thought they were two people eager to get inside. Well, I suppose I did think it was odd, but not odd enough to get involved, but strange all the same. Even more so as the man looked familiar to me and a lot older than the woman he was encouraging inside. That man is now sitting over there beside the window."

Becky turned around to see who Colin was talking about. She recognised the gentleman at once. "That's Henry Phillips, the groom's dad."

Chapter 8

There was a part of Martin that felt uncertain about walking into a church on a Sunday. Stepping through the lychgate and approaching the arched doors over uneven paving stones, dragged up dark memories from his childhood. Back then, when he was home from boarding school, Sunday morning church services were a fact of life, there was no escape. It wearied him to the point of one day faking a leg injury after breakfast. Even though his mother could see no sign of any damage to his ankle but for the howls of faked pain as she examined it, his father suggested that he stay at home for the rest of the day. The gardener was around on a Sunday and would keep an eye on the boy. Mother was not so sure, but she acquiesced and after putting an ice pack on his ankle sent him to his room to rest.

Flushed with success Martin settled down on his bed to play Super Mario on his Nintendo. Already he was wondering just what sort of excuse he could come up with next week to avoid any boring religious homilies. As he navigated Mario through the on-screen kingdoms, his mind was far away, when his mother called, "Martin, I have some fresh baked oat cookies, still hot out of the oven."

His favourite and still hot. This was turning out to be the perfect Sunday. It was only as he reached the bottom of the stairs in record time, that he recalled Mother was getting ready for church, not cooking. He was right. She stood at the bottom of the stairs in her finest church outfit.

"Looks like we have a miracle on our hands Martin. You had best come to church and give thanks."

As Martin opened the door for Susan, he consoled himself with the fact that this church was nothing like the others he had visited. How bad could it be, a room full of eccentrics who wanted to live in a bygone age, just like any other church he guessed.

After all it was going to be a birthday party, at least that was how Dave Harvey had described the event. Like all good parties, this one had a bouncer at the door to maintain security and to keep the rabble out. It was no surprise to see he was dressed as a Roman centurion in full armour, holding a shield and wearing a skirt, although Martin did recall from his time at school that it was called a tunica. The security guard was even wearing a cassis on his head; he was ready to defend the Roman Empire at all costs. The only downside was he was clearly of Chinese origin and was scarcely five feet tall. The advantage of his diminutive height was that he could hide his complete body behind his large rectangular ornate shield.

"Who doth enter these hallowed halls of mighty Jupiter?"

"Dave Harvey invited us," Susan replied, as if seeing a five-feet high Chinese Roman soldier was an everyday occurrence in her life.

"What reason, thou knave? Thou naughty knave, what reason?"

Martin picked up that the guard was clearly well versed in Shakespeare, even if he did have a strong American accent.

Martin and Susan looked at each other before Susan continued, "We're guests, personal guests of Mr Harvey, he invited us."

The centurion looked suspiciously at Martin, whose face reflected the surprise of seeing such an unusual security guard who sounded as if he was born in Shakespeare's era.

"Know I this man that comes along with you?"

"He's called Martin."

The guard shook his head as he stared at Martin before pointing out, "You have such a February face, so full of frost, of storm and cloudiness. Thine face is not worth sunburning."

"Are you trying to insult me in Shakespearean prose?" Martin queried.

"You have a plentiful lack of wit. Away you three-inch fool. Martin and his fair maiden, Jupiter awaits you. Have a nice day."

With a flourish the short Roman Soldier opened the inner door and ushered them into the church, now technically a temple.

What yesterday had been a cavernous empty space was now occupied with a large number of people standing around, chatting, holding plates of food, goblets of drink, all seemed to be relaxed and enjoying the soiree.

Apart from the large statue of Jupiter at one end of the temple or church, however you wanted to describe it, the gathering could be just like any other social event one might be invited to. Along the right-hand side of the hall were tables covered with red paper, laden with plates of food and drink. Behind the table, replenishing drinks and serving food were three men, dressed in what appeared to be drab hessian sacks. They were the first clue that this was not your typical English gathering.

Also the attendees could be divided into those who were dressed like any modern Europeans, such as Susan and

Martin, then there were those who dressed in the fashion of ancient Rome, togas, tunics and open-toed sandals.

"Well," Susan said, "might as well join in the fun. Let's get a drink." Without waiting for a reply, she scurried over to one of the tables and grabbed a plastic wine glass, clearly a modern world thing, took a swig, then immediately screwed up her face from the vile taste. She swallowed it in one go before replacing the empty glass back on the table.

"That's vile; do all Romans drink this sweet rubbish?"

The man in the hessian sack smiled.

"It's called Mulsum, regular wine with added honey. I should try one of those drinks," he pointed to a line of plastic glasses with a mixture of white and red liquids in them.

"Wine watered down a little as the Romans would have done. A lot more palatable than Mulsum."

Susan selected a white wine, emptied the whole glass in one go to clear out the taste of the honey. Then she picked up another glass, before turning her attention to the food on offer.

"The Romans had a wide range of often weird food, including flamingo and dormouse," the attendant began to explain helpfully, not having seen Susan at the temple before. "Dormice are off the menu because they are a protected species and flamingos are in short supply in this part of Grantham. We just pop down to Lidl and get a shed load of party food. Nothing scary on the table I can assure you." He leaned towards Susan and murmured, "It's the dressing up we all like."

Having chosen a soft drink as he was driving, Martin and Susan moved towards the throng that milled around, unsure of who they should speak to or what questions they should ask, when they heard a voice address them,

"No doubt our senator Mr Harvey invited you to experience a Roman dies natalis."

It was Leon the lanky cleaner from yesterday, the computer expert, who now stood in front of them holding a tray of drinks. Dressed in the hessian uniform of a pleb, he was serving those around him.

"If you need any introductions to anyone or have any questions, I can help you. I think you'll find that we are all very average and boring here. We're not inclined to burn down our neighbours or even throw anyone to the lions."

"Yet you still have a guard on the door?" Martin pointed out.

"You mean Eric Chow, I would not really consider him a guard, his height is against him, as is his naturally placid nature. He just likes the idea of dressing up in the uniform of a Roman soldier. As Mr Harvey, our senator, does not like to see swords and uniforms at such a social gathering, we leave him at the door, which suits Eric fine."

"What's with his weird Shakespearean quotes? I thought Americans were not that keen on the Bard," Martin queried.

"Eric Chow is not American," Leon explained. "He arrived here from China about three years ago, he's never been to the States. His use of the English language is self-taught, which he is very proud of. Sadly, for us, the only books he had to hand were the complete works of Shakespeare and then he relied on Netflix to help him learn the language. I always think of him as an example of: what if William Shakespeare was born in Stratford, Connecticut?"

"How is this all paid for?" Martin asked bluntly, after all he was there to find out more about the church and not, as Susan downed her third glass of wine, enjoy himself.

"Partly contributions from those you see around you. We all pay a moderate annual subscription, not much more than any other social club you might wish to belong to. The temple income is then subsidised by the profits from the Roman shop that Mr Harvey operates, mainly online sales. He does well out of online sales. I know that as I have helped him with tweaking the site to optimise it."

"How do you optimise a website?" Martin asked hoping that he would understand the answer.

"Making certain the metadata is working well on the website enabling it to get to the top of all the search engines. Ensuring the customer experience is free flowing once they are on the site, as well as making sure that the not so good reviews are tucked away somewhere."

"That last bit sounds shady."

"Well one bad review in a hundred could, if it was in your face, affect sales, so I just ensure that they, the bad ones, are always a few reviews down the page. Lots of companies do exactly the same, it's all part of the game. But don't just take my word for it, ask around, speak to people, we have nothing to hide, and you'll soon understand that the allegations that that plonker Rodney has made are baseless."

The next hour was spent drinking, talking, drinking and talking, as well as drinking. As parties went, Susan was most impressed with this one. Although the wine, by their own admission, was watered down, she still enjoyed it.

"Tell me," Susan leaned closer to Martin, "you're a detective of sorts, do you think that these men are wearing their underpants?"

"Does it really matter?"

"No, I just always wonder the same question when I see men in togas or kilts. Are they going commando or not?"

"Colin wears a skirt, why not ask him?"

"That's not the same or even appropriate. Clearly you have no idea. I'm going to get another drink." Susan hurried off towards the man in the hessian outfit.

Martin felt there was a clear distinction in the room. After speaking to several of the congregation, those taking part fell into two different groups. The first group were those who had an obsession with the defunct Roman Empire and all things related to the times. Generally, they were the ones in togas, trying their best to drop a few Latin words into their conversations.

The second group were those who viewed the gatherings as a social event, a chance to meet people. They enjoyed the pomp and circumstance yet shied away from taking part in the rituals. The second group were also the ones who overall retained their modern attire. The one thing they all had in common was their love of the temple, their fellow worshippers, and Mr Harvey, a kind, generous man, who according to many of his followers, put a lot of hard work into the whole place.

As Susan returned with her full glass, Dave Harvey joined them displaying a beaming smile. He was dressed in a smart toga with purple edging, a scroll of some sort in his hand and a garland of laurel leaves on his head. A pendant, resembling a seal of office hung around his neck on a leather cord. He had the swagger of a leader of his people, which suited him well.

"I'm pleased you could make it. I have seen you talking to some of the members, all of whom I am sure have reassured you that we are a peace-loving group of people, not a terrorist sect wanting to re-establish the power and might of the Roman Empire.

"I am off to do a bit of official work. Please stay as long as you wish and talk to anyone and everyone, I have nothing to hide."

Martin watched as Senator Harvey melted into the crowd, before posing a question to Susan. "I know I said I like the man. But. How many times does he need to say he has nothing to hide..."

"...unless he has something to hide," Susan finished the sentence. She pointed towards a man dressed in a toga eating a picnic-size scotch egg. "He might have the answer."

Without any form of polite introduction or even a smile, Susan questioned the man, who was about to pop another scotch egg into his mouth.

"Are you left-handed?"

If Scotch egg man was being honest that was not the sort of question he often heard. Occasionally if he was signing a document in front of someone who did not know him, they would comment on him being left-handed. He had never been asked about his dexterity at a party before.

"Yes, why do you ask?" he queried in case they were from the hand police.

In fact, it was exactly the same question that Martin wanted to ask Susan.

"Well, I thought," Susan pointed to his hand, "that Romans thought being left-handed was unlucky."

He nodded in agreement. "Absolutely. Back in the day, us lefties were looked upon as being evil creatures. Lucky for me I didn't live in those times."

"But Rodney was thrown out of the church because he was left-handed."

"Ah." Scotch egg man put down his paper plate, saving one that was about to roll onto the table. He sounded and looked embarrassed to be asked such a question. "That was the excuse they used, the public excuse. Everyone here was told it was to do with unacceptable behaviour in the temple, which left everyone wanting to know more. Well, it would, wouldn't it, we all like scandal as long as it doesn't involve us. If I could tell you more I would; I hate having secrets." He picked up his plate once more and popped a scotch egg into his mouth with his left hand.

As much as Martin was taking things easy, he told Susan to finish her drink so they should make their way back to the hotel as it was time for them to get ready to follow the barmaid's husband. But first, Martin needed the toilet, something that he was going to regret as it would be etched into his memory for years to come.

***

Off to the right of Jupiter's statue was a small plain door with the internationally accepted signs for the lavatories, a man and woman standing beside each other. On the other side of the door was a short narrow corridor, at the end of which was a door to the left and another to the right. The door on the right side had the word: 'feminae', obviously the ladies, Martin concluded. The other door: 'hominum' Martin pushed open, not registering that left-handed doors could also be unlucky.

It was a square room, with a small window set high on the wall at the far end. On that wall were three hand basins, a hand dryer and a mirror below the window. On both the left and right-hand walls were four toilets, not urinals, but proper sit-down toilets. They had no doors, no partitions, no privacy. Just eight toilets facing the centre of the room with two of them already occupied by men sitting down, one with his toga around his waist, the other, his jeans and pants around his ankles. Martin was shocked at what he saw, as well as being unable to understand the process which would enable him to relieve his bladder.

The man in the toga looked up at Martin, grinned widely as he spoke to welcome the newest visitor to the Roman gents.

"Your first time in a latrina, take a seat. It's all easy really, as well as being very sociable."

Martin was not convinced that going to the toilet could be considered a sociable event. Lunch at a restaurant, dinner at the Savoy, theatre, opera, even at a push, the cinema, they could be considered social occasions. Sitting on a porcelain toilet with your trousers around your ankles was not, in Martin's opinion, a social event. The problem was, he did need to answer the call of nature and even with a very fast exit from the temple, followed by a hasty drive back to the hotel, it might not be a short enough time to deal with the feeling in his bladder. Reluctantly, he undid his belt, lowered his clothing from below his waist and coyly sat down.

The man in the toga called out, "Just be thankful these are not the rough wooden benches the real Romans had to endure." He then returned to his conversation with his friend, leaving Martin to go about his business.

Even in the somewhat unusual situation, Martin managed to relieve his bladder and listen to the two men talking at the same time. The modern-dressed man was moaning while his toga-dressed friend nodded in agreement.

"I wouldn't mind, but every Monday he wants me to go through a load of stock that he has picked up over the weekend. Then I have to take a picture of each item and stick it on the website. All that and he expects it to be up online the same evening."

"What even all the little Roman coins?"

"Yeah, well at least they are clean, but he tells me each one is a unique item, although they all look the same to me. It's them bracelets that are a pain, but they are not original, he knows they're fake, well, replicas should I say, that's the polite way of putting it."

"So, he gets all his stuff from the dealer during the weekend. I still think he must have good contacts to get so much. I know when I was collecting Roman items, good stuff was few and far between. I know the bracelets and brooches are replicas, but the coins, well they are meant to be the real McCoy."

"As I said, every Monday he plonks a box load of the stuff in my house and I get listing. To be honest, they are a real faff, but he bungs me a few quid, so it helps the pension."

Realising that the two men were just chatting and not doing what they were meant to in the toilet, Martin stood up, re-dressed, washed his hands and left the room wishing both men a good one, which he regretted saying as soon as he had said it.

***

"Let me get this straight, you heard this through a number of walls in the toilet?" Susan asked.

"No, I told you there were no walls." Martin changed gear annoyed that Susan seemed unable to comprehend the men's toilets at the temple.

"But then it is like having a shit in the living room."

"Not exactly, unless your living room has a number of toilets placed around it."

"But it's not natural to poo in public."

"I know that, you know that, but apparently the ancient Romans had a very different approach to bodily functions."

"Well, I am just glad I did not need to use the facilities. I think I'd be too embarrassed to go in that situation."

Martin wanted to move away from bodily functions. Instead, he recalled the conversation he had heard for Susan, before adding his own theory. Considering that Edwin had wondered just how Dave Harvey managed to get such a regular supply of artefacts, and Martin had heard that every Monday new stock came in, something was not right. Although he did not want to admit that Dave Harvey might be up to no good, he was beginning to think that could very well be the case.

Chapter 9

It was ten minutes before six o'clock. On each side of the narrow road, electric lights began to go on in the terraced houses as families prepared for the evening. In his car, Martin and Susan were waiting patiently for the door of number seven to open. Then they would get their first look at the husband suspected of dalliance. It was not long before they saw the upstairs lights go out, then soon after the downstairs lights too. Shortly after, the door of number seven opened and a man stepped out into the street.

"He looks like the man Imogen described," Martin confirmed as he started the engine of his car preparing to follow the small grey Ford Fiesta that the man had just got into.

"That's good to hear. I was worried that your barmaid might have a harem of men in her house."

"I don't think you can have a harem of men," Martin pointed out, "not that I am sure what a group of such men would be called."

"I'll Google it." Susan entered the query into her phone as Martin pulled out of his parking place and began to follow the Fiesta. "Wow, that is some hulk, look." She thrust the phone in front of Martin's face.

"Susan! I'm driving," pushing her hand away. "Why are you showing me photos of semi-naked men?"

"I thought you might be interested to see what a male harem is called. Not that I've found out yet, but I'm having fun looking. My God, that six-pack is giving me the shakes. Here have a look."

Again, Susan thrust the phone in front of Martin, who once more pointed out that he was driving and in no position to look at soft porn on her phone. He added that even if he was not driving, he would still not be in the least interested in it.

Fortunately, on a Sunday evening the traffic around the outskirts of Grantham was light, which enabled Martin to follow the barmaid's husband with ease. Susan settled back down to researching the name for a male harem by looking at men in various stages of disrobement. In silence, they followed the Fiesta for almost ten minutes before the small, grey-coloured car pulled into a fenced-off car park of what looked to be a local community hall. The husband meticulously checked each door was locked, folded back the door mirrors and adjusted his jacket, before he walked away from his car. Martin parked opposite and watched him stride confidently into the building.

Susan looked up. "Well, I didn't expect that. Do you reckon he meets his bit of stuff in there, then they go off to a pub or something?" Susan asked, bored of looking at semi-naked men in her quest to find the correct description for a male harem.

"If he does, then that must be the strangest location to carry out a clandestine love affair. We should walk over and see what's going on in there. I am thinking maybe it's the local amateur dramatics group. Yet, he looked smartly dressed, so maybe it's a formal reception, dinner, drinks."

They left the car and crossed the quiet side road towards the closed double doors. There was a sign on the metal fence which surrounded the hall and protected it from the outside world. 'The Greta Norman Memorial Hall' was a tired looking building that had seen better days, yet still managed to serve faithfully the community in which it had been placed. Susan hoped that Greta Norman, whoever she might have been, was still proud of the service the hall could provide. They both tried to peer in through the glass windows, all of which were frosted and gave no clue as to the activity going on inside. All they could hear was music; there were no vocals only a slow beat.

"Let's go in," Susan whispered and pushed open the door, which led them into a small vestibule. The music was now louder. There was a toilet door on each side of them and the floor was stained from years of use. On their left was a noticeboard with a selection of notices pinned to it: a scout group, a choral society, an amateur dramatic company called the Grantham Grannies and ballroom dancing classes. Ahead of them was another set of double doors behind which the music had now stopped. They waited in silence, unsure if they should push the next set of doors open. The same song played again. Susan's inquisitiveness got the better of her; she gently pushed open one of the doors ever so slightly, hoping to get just enough vision to see what activity was going on in the hall.

Before she had opened the door a crack, it was pulled away from her hands and opened wide into the hall. A short man with grey hair and neatly trimmed, equally grey moustache stood in front of her. Both he and Susan jumped back in surprise.

"Jesus, you gave me a start." He looked at Susan and then turned towards Martin. "There's no need to be shy; come in and join us, the more the merrier, whatever your standard."

Martin and Susan stood in the now fully open doorway; several pairs of eyes were looking at them. The hall was populated with couples, their arms locked as they embraced each other. They had almost all stopped dancing to see who Clifford, the man with the grey hair, had discovered loitering at the door. A tall woman, standing beside a record player, called to them,

"Don't be bashful, we are here for all levels of ballroom dancing, beginner or expert. First and foremost, we're here to enjoy ourselves. Come in, join us." She waved her arm to encourage the newcomers onto the dance floor.

As if they had been hypnotised, Susan and Martin walked into the hall. The door banged closed behind them; they were now trapped in a ballroom dance class.

"I'm Tracey and I'm the teacher here. Have either of you ever danced before?"

"A simple waltz is about my level of dancing," Susan confessed, having only shaken her body around a pile of handbags in a dance club while being inebriated. This was going to be very different.

"I'm sorry we got the wrong day; we thought it was the Am Dram night," Martin found himself saying, planning to turn and head out as soon as possible.

"Don't be silly, anyone can do a waltz and if your young lady can waltz, then just grab her in your arms and we'll begin. Just follow my steps. Right class once more." Tracey pressed the play button on the CD player and the class of dancers began to waltz around the room.

Tracey immediately paid attention to her newcomers, guiding Martin, who she quickly noticed could dance, he just had not wanted to admit it. In her words, Martin had natural rhythm, which he was fully aware of having previously thrown himself into dancing Salsa to satisfy the whim of one of his ex-girlfriends. After the third song, with a few words of encouragement and with only a slight adjustment to Martin's frame, Tracey was happy to move onto another couple.

Tracey was in her thirties, tall, with jet black hair, long legs and a slender body. Her face was triangular with a snub nose and teeth that had even gaps between them. Her eyes were narrow and deep-set. It was her hands that concerned Susan as she handled Martin's body to encourage him to carry out the right steps. They were grimy as if she was employed elsewhere as an engineer or mechanic, not the hands you would expect of a dance teacher.

As Martin held Susan close in his arms, counting the musical beats: one, two, three in his head, Susan asked him a question.

"What aftershave are you wearing?"

"I don't recall the name exactly."

Martin's confession troubled Susan. She knew full well that he was very particular about his aftershave. He might have a selection available to him, but even so, he would know which one he was wearing at any time. The reason she was interested was based on her previous experience of taking in the aroma of his aftershave. He had a preference for three, the one that she was inhaling now was none of those three. Worse than that, it was one she was pretty sure she knew.

"Why are you wearing Kouros? That is not one of your regular brands, is it?"

"Does it matter now? I'm trying to keep my feet in time with the music, so not a good time to ask me a trivial question." Dancing a salsa was one thing, doing a simple waltz was for some reason beyond the current skill level of his feet.

"Colin wears Kouros."

"Does he?" Martin replied looking down at his feet, willing them into the right spot.

"Why are you wearing Colin's aftershave? Don't tell me you have forgotten yours, that's just not believable."

"I'm sharing a room with Colin," Martin admitted. "I was not paying attention; I was in a rush. You recall we were late back from the Roman party; hence I ended up splashing his Kouros all over. Simple error, the bathroom was a little overcrowded as well; you would not believe how much make-up he has spread around."

Susan stopped dancing and held Martin at arm's length. "You're sleeping with Colin?"

She did not mean for it to sound the way it came out. If she had qualified her statement with the fact that it was better than sleeping in the staff quarters of the hotel, it might have sounded better.

As she hadn't, all the other dance pupils only heard 'you're sleeping with Colin', which in their minds, not knowing either of the two newcomers, translated to some poor young woman discovering that her boyfriend has turned out to be gay.

Fortunately, Martin was too preoccupied with explaining to Susan the exact circumstances for the reason he ended up in Colin's room to notice the sympathetic looks she was getting. The other plus point for him was, as he was explaining it all to her, his mind let his feet do their own thing and they were becoming very accomplished at the waltz without him looking at them.

Susan pulled Martin close to her and smiled. "You've had a very traumatic weekend so far; let's hope there aren't too many more cultural shocks for you."

He had to agree that he had seen some things that he would prefer to forget. Yet there were other things that he was enjoying, including holding Susan in his arms, feeling her body next to his as they moved around the dance floor in harmony. Her perfume, her warmth, her humour, he loved them all.

There was a large part of him that wanted to take Susan seriously and ask her for a real date. Not a work dinner, or a bite to eat, a real date, begin a relationship. That last thought gave him a sense of unease.

He had had relationships before. Young women, older women, socially acceptable girlfriends, others who were frowned upon. All relationships, for whatever reason ended, none of them on good terms. Each one had brought their own amount of trouble and anguish into his life. He was no longer on talking terms with any of them, which is to be expected and in the long-term generally for the best. That was the real reason he was holding back asking Susan for a romantic liaison. He would hate to be in a place where he never saw or spoke to her again. Plus, how difficult would it be, if after a failed attempt at being a couple, she then decided to remain as a director. On that basis, he would just close down the detective agency, well, it never really existed until Becky made it into a limited company, with he and Susan as joint directors.

If he had a choice, he was going to play the safe game. Stay joint directors, stay friends, stay talking, stay laughing and enjoy her company. Romance and sex he imagined could spoil everything, or make it even better, a small insurgent voice whispered in his head.

When the foxtrot began, Susan and Martin decided to sit it out. Together they took a seat at the edge of the dance floor where some others watched in envy, as more competent pupils glided around.

Clifford walked over and sat down next to Susan. "Not seen you two around before, plus you don't sound local to me; new to the area?"

"Just up for the weekend, a friend's wedding," Susan answered, not keen to engage in any lengthy conversation with him; he smelt peculiar. It was not an unpleasant aroma, not an unwashed body odour, it was a more weird than disagreeable one. Clifford, on the other hand, being unaware of his smell, was happy to chat until the next dance style was initiated.

"What brings you to Tracey's dance class?"

It was a fair question that Susan had no reasonable explanation for. Well, she did have a reason, it was just that she did not want to share it. Instead, she used her initiative.

"Martin can explain that better than I can." She turned to a surprised looking Martin, who felt the eyes of both Clifford and Susan looking at him for an answer, which he did not have to hand.

"You're asking why we happened upon this very local dance class when we were yesterday at a friend's wedding and planning to leave the area in the morning? It might seem strange to anyone outside of our circle." Martin paused, he didn't think being honest and saying they were watching one of the dancers to see if he was having an affair was the best response. His actual reply was not much better, "The groom's father, Mr Phillips, suggested we visit; he had seen me dancing and suggested I needed dance classes."

If Clifford, or for that matter anyone else listening to the conversation, was going to be logical, they would have pointed out 'why go to a dance class at least one hundred miles from where you live? Wouldn't it be better to wait until you are home then look for a local dance class?' Of course, that was going to be the best option. However,

Clifford missed that obvious fact and latched onto the name of Mr Phillips.

"Henry Phillips, of course, his son got married yesterday; you must have been one of his guests. Never got an invite, too far down the pecking order am I, only a vague business acquaintance."

"You know Henry Phillips?" Susan asked.

"Everyone, well at least those of us in the business community, knows Henry Phillips. One of those men who are always there to help and support fledgeling companies in the area. I have a great deal of respect for the man. Helped me out a lot when my business, selling poultry…"

Ah, Susan thought, that was the odour.

"…was taking a downturn and I was having trouble paying my bills. Being a member of the local chamber of commerce, Henry was on hand to offer advice. Helped me out, found a tenant for the flat above my shop; not everyone wants to live above a poultry shop; certainly, he made a huge difference at the time."

"He is a butcher, not an estate agent?" Martin queried.

"Maybe, but he has lots of useful contacts. He found a couple of women who did not mind the odours my shop emits. They seemed happy, pleasant enough, but don't see much of them; they do keep themselves to themselves. Ah, the quickstep is next."

Clifford stood up, straightened his striped tie, pulled his shirt sleeves down and shook the creases out of his trousers. He looked down at the two interlopers from London.

"Of course, you are at the Harby Hall Hotel. Reggie, over there in the pink shirt," Clifford pointed to a man who was talking to his partner at the end of the dance, "his wife works there, in the bar, I think. Sweet really, they're having a celebration for their thirtieth wedding anniversary, and he's here in secret. Going to surprise his old girl by dancing around the dance floor with her. Never done that the whole time they've been married."

"Surprise his wife?" Susan asked.

"Yes, by all accounts she loves dancing, whereas poor old Reggie there, has always thought he's got two left feet. Well, she's in for a big surprise when he whisks her up in his arms and whirls her around the dance floor; shame we can't go and see it. Music's starting, best find a partner for my dance. Nice talking to you both."

Martin turned to Susan, a large grin on his face. He had come up trumps. There was no affair, a simple surprise for his wife, end of investigation. Hence, he concluded, "we might as well go back to the hotel, have a drink and tell Imogen that she will need to act surprised when her husband floats across the dance floor towards her. Our mission is complete." Martin stood and was at once roughly pulled back down by Susan.

"Not so fast."

"Am I missing something here?"

"You're being naïve Martin, as always. Reggie, the wayward husband, isn't going to arrive at this dance group announcing that he's here to have an affair. The dance class could well be a cover. I am thinking we stay to the end of the evening, see who he leaves the dance with?"

"Your thinking is over thinking Susan, as always. Have you seen the standard of females here tonight? Apart from you, there is no one to fancy. Let's get back; I need a drink."

"Martin, you are young and handsome, Reggie is old, grey haired, has a bit of a bloated belly, and that's apart from his crooked teeth, so he can't afford to be fussy. It's a good bet that he will leave here tonight with one of the middle-aged female dancers."

"We are waiting until the end, aren't we?" Martin asked knowing full well Susan's answer.

It was not all bad for him; he did get to dance with Susan for most of the night, and almost managed to get his feet to follow the steps required for a jive. As working evenings go, he enjoyed this one. That was until the end when Susan insisted that they stay in their parked car and watch Reggie return to his vehicle, no doubt, Susan was convinced, with a female partner.

The plan did not work out exactly as hoped. Reggie did leave the hall as expected, watched by Martin and Susan. He walked to his car, carefully wiped the evening moisture from the door mirrors. He sat in the car for a few minutes; Martin suggested to warm it up before moving off. Susan still believed he was waiting for a liaison. A moment or two later, Reggie drove off alone. It was the fact that Martin rubbed in her misjudgement, that annoyed Susan even more than being wrong.

Just as Martin started his engine preparing to drive back to the hotel, Susan urged him to stay parked right where he was and look over towards the hall entrance. They watched Tracey carefully lock the double doors, shaking them to ensure they were secure and then make her way to a waiting car, a big Mercedes that had been parked outside. Neither of them could see the driver clearly, they did however recognise the personalised number plate. Tracey got into the car and was driven away by Dave Harvey.

***

"Do you know how long you take in the bathroom?" Martin asked, as Colin exited dressed in a blue candlewick dressing gown. Martin had been resting on his single bed, waiting patiently for his turn to clean his teeth before turning in for the night. The hiatus of waiting for Colin had given him time to think, something he tried to avoid where possible.

Generally, when you have to think about something, it means there are options and choices to be made. Martin preferred to go with the flow, see what turned up, deal with it, then move on. There was no point in worrying about things that you could not control. That was the idea until Colin had spent the best part of half an hour in the bathroom going through his pre-slumber routine.

"You sound just like my ex-wife; she was always complaining. To be fair Martin, you have very little idea about the trials and tribulations of removing layers of foundation and make-up. My ex-wife on the other hand should have realised that such things take time, yet she still complained."

"Why does marriage so often end up in heartache and disappointment?"

It was a question that had been niggling at Martin all evening. Laying on the bed waiting for Colin, that niggling thought had become a significant concern. Vera, dumping her marriage for the delights of being a cannabis-smoking environmentalist. Imogen the barmaid, having cosmetic surgery, maybe to try and recapture the attention of her husband. Even though he was innocent, and she was happy to hear that he was planning to spin her around the dance floor for a surprise, she still appeared to have doubts and fears.

In his simple world, when you love someone, you trust them all the time. Why was marriage so complex? As a young man, he had an innocent vision of two people getting married, being deeply in love and spending the rest of their lives in bliss. That vision had been shattered when former girlfriend Paula, took him for a ride, swindling thousands of pounds out of him. It had never been about the money for him, it was the betrayal that hurt.

Even his own parents, who never separated before the death of his father, were always at loggerheads with each other. What happens to the love two people must have when they get married? Maybe that is when the rot sets in, at the very start of a marriage.

Howard wanted a small wedding; his parents had forced him to have a big lavish affair. The parents argued over the catering, the decorations, the guests. Maybe that is the first crack, when the newlyweds must take on the anguish of their parents. But if marriage was that difficult, why do it in the first place?

"You're asking me? You do realise that I am a previously married, now happily divorced person. I am not a shining example of the marriage machine you know."

"I know that, but why did you and your wife fall out of love? You must have loved each other when you first got married."

Colin sat down on the bed where Martin was stretched out, his hands behind his head, resting the intense activity that was going on inside.

"Is Martin getting all broody being at a wedding, is that it?"

"No, it is why, after so many years you were married, you suddenly decide to part from your wife."

Colin rolled back the years to the time when he was a young man. Yes, he had loved his wife back then. Fell head over heels in love with his northern rose. He met her at the time he had been deployed as a young constable to Easington in County Durham, during the miners' strike. She had been buying groceries, tripped and sprained her ankle. The attractive London constable carried her shopping and supported her back to her small, terraced house. Colin thought of it as mutually falling in love.

They got over the resistance of her family to her marrying a southerner which was marginally better than taking a policeman as her spouse. Within a year they were walking down the aisle together. The following year their first son was born; two years later their second boy arrived.

Living in marital bliss, Colin went about his day job policing the streets of south London. His wife, once the children had both started school, found herself a part-time job in a bank. They appeared to be and believed they were the perfect couple, raising their children as best they could, loving each other whenever the opportunity arose.

Unnoticed by either of them, a small space began to appear between them as their lives began to deviate. Colin learnt too late that being married was all about sharing the same life, not living one's own life. For Colin there was his job; promotion to a detective seemed a good idea, until the countless hours of overtime that were forced upon him left him with fewer hours to spend with his wife and children.

Then there came a moment when in the despondency of endless work, he tried lipstick for the first time. He often reflected on those days and the choices he made. His work was often dangerous, always stressful, totally consuming all his energy.

Unable to share all the depressing and brutal details of his work with his wife, led to her lack of understanding of what he was going through. She could not comprehend what was happening to him as he lurched towards a crisis not all of his own making.

Other colleagues faced similar dilemmas. Some took to alcohol; some took to drugs, in order to escape the pressure cooker lives they were leading. One took his own life to escape the maelstrom.

Colin found his own escape was to wear women's clothes. Maybe if he had drunk excessively then his wife might have accepted that. Having a husband who dressed as a woman was too much for her. The love they once had finally eroded away through circumstances they had little control over.

The divorce came more than a decade ago. Colin left the force and even though he no longer had the stresses and pressures of being a detective, he continued to hide his damaged memories behind the female clothes that became his trademark. He felt less vulnerable, better able to cope with life.

"Growing old together is the key to a successful marriage, Martin." Colin said thoughtfully. "But you need to understand that growing old does not start when you retire. It starts the moment you say, 'I do'. From then on, you must share your life, mature together, grow together, always moving in the same direction, together. My wife and I, through no fault of our own, well, maybe we were not observant enough, ended up treading different pathways. I didn't love her any less when I divorced her than I did when I married her. It was just we were, by that time, both totally different people."

"Marriage sounds tough to me; maybe in the end it's not worth all the bother?"

"Life can be described as a bother. The problem is we don't really know where life is going to lead us. I wouldn't change marrying my wife and having two fine boys. And being a transvestite, I will admit, did contribute to the divorce. On the other hand, it led to me helping Suzie Baby get out of a situation with some nasty blokes. That in turn led me to sitting on a bed with you. That sounds a little weird, I know, but you get my point. Until we take our last breath on this earth, we have no idea where the currents of life will take us. I think the best thing to do is not swim against the tide, go with the flow and see where you end up. Isn't that one of your sayings?"

Colin stood up from the bed and walked over to the minibar, took out two miniatures of gin, then held them up above his head.

"If you're getting broody and looking for a relationship story that will end in happy ever after, then you're out of luck. No relationship, however great it might seem, ever ends well. If you're lucky enough for the relationship to go full term, then one of you will die and the other will be left alone. There's no such thing as happy ever after, just heartbreak and tears.

"Now let's move on from feeling sorry for ourselves. I can't go to sleep with all these deep philosophical thoughts rolling around my head. Let's have a drink and you tell me about the dance class."

Chapter 10

As much as the dance class story mildly interested Colin, the fact that the straying husband was not in fact straying and instead was going to show an act of tacky romance to his wife, did nothing to stimulate him. He had hoped that Imogen's husband was conducting an illicit affair that would mean Martin had to gather some evidence. Getting Martin to do some work was what Colin really wanted.

The fire, allegedly started by Jupiter, the God not the dog, was of much more interest and worthy of the cheapest tabloid newspaper. Colin wanted to know more and once the minibar had been emptied, room service provided a bottle of red wine and two glasses. The conversation continued as Martin explained what happened during his visit to Rodney and the circumstances of the fire.

"But he couldn't have done it himself; he told you he was at work," Colin concluded. "You can't start a fire when you are driving a bus around Grantham."

As Martin poured a glass of wine for himself and topped up Colin's glass, he pointed out that he had seen films where it was possible to set up some sort of apparatus that delayed the start of the fire. Even though he could not exactly recall the film, he had seen it and was confident it could be done, even if the insurance company had found no such contraption.

The counter claim to that was Colin's insistence that Martin's theory was poppycock. Greed is, in the main, the root cause of crime. The church wanting the land to expand their operations was motive enough in Colin's mind for them to force poor Rodney into a position where he would have to sell the house.

Although the alcohol was clouding Martin's thought development, he did point out that even Rodney had admitted without his mother, he could not afford to run the house. It would have made perfect sense after his mother died for Rodney to look at ways of cashing in on the asset he could not afford. Burning it down for the insurance money was a good way forward.

Not in the least convinced by Martin's reasoning, Colin stepped up the attack by referring to another fact that Rodney had shared with Martin, 'Rodney bought a large caravan to rent out before the fire, that must have cost a pretty penny.'

This Martin turned to his advantage. "It could have been that he bought it with a loan that he had secured with the house. Then by burning the house down, he gets the insurance money and has a place to stay when the house has gone. All looking very much pre-planned to my mind."

"But," Colin once again pointed out, "Rodney was at work when the fire started. The insurance company found nothing like an advanced fire starter system that you see in films. A shady guy, Dave Harvey, it's still my firm belief that he's somehow connected to the fire that destroyed Rodney's house."

"No, not in my books." Martin finished his glass of wine. "Dave Harvey seemed a genuine sort of bloke; spiteful people who are jealous of him start rumours and the whole thing snowballs."

"Martin you are such a snob. Just because the man has money and a big house, you think he's all okay. But the poor common bus driver, he'll have no qualms about defrauding the insurance company."

"You sound just like Susan. I'm not a snob, I am just telling you how I see it. I met both Rodney and Dave and I've seen the house. I conclude as the detective, Rodney is my prime suspect. Dave might have a dubious side to him, but I doubt he is an arsonist."

"That's it!" Colin exclaimed in an unusually aggressive manner for him. "As a real ex-detective, I want to see for myself and then I, using my years of experience, will come up with the solution."

Colin stood up and took his coat from the wardrobe, then opened his phone.

"Sit down Miss Marple, it is the middle of the night and I doubt either Rodney or Dave will welcome us calling on them."

"They might not relish our visit, but the house has no say in the matter and is neither awake nor asleep and certainly not occupied. We'll go to the house and I'll use my wide experiences from my time in the force to ascertain the cause of the fire."

"You are not a forensic fire investigator."

"No, but I have seen plenty of fires, both accidental and deliberate. I have a pretty good idea as to what to look for. We're going there tonight. End of, get your coat."

Martin flopped back on the bed. He was tired, had a little too much to drink and was sure that come the morning things would look clearer to Colin. He pointed out that neither of them was in a fit state to drive. Let's get some sleep, he suggested, as Colin began changing into his day clothes.

"I am fully aware both of us are over the limit, so I am calling an Uber."

"You got the munchies now? If you are ordering food, I will have some sort of hummus and bread."

Looking down at Martin on the bed, Colin slowly shook his head, sometimes Martin's lack of life experiences slightly worried him.

"Not Uber Eats, you posh talking fool, I'm getting ourselves a cab to take us to Rodney's house. Put your coat on; it'll be here in three minutes."

***

Sobhy Khaled drove his Kia Niro with pride. He congratulated himself on always having a clean and tidy car. He was one of the most diligent Uber drivers in the area when it came to presentation. A booking just after one in the morning, he would be circumspect as to whether he would accept the request. But from the Harby Hall Hotel going to Branston Road, both decent areas, he had few reservations about accepting the request from Colin Higgins. On balance it seemed good.

Sobhy had not always been as cautious. When he lived in Syria with his wife and two-year-old daughter, everything felt familiar. He and his family were living in a war zone, a fact that did not concern him too much; he was used to the conditions and carried on his usual daily routine. Until one day he returned from work just as a stray artillery shell landed on his house. He scrambled through the wreckage, frantically pulling the lifeless body of his daughter from the dust and rubble then stumbling across parts of his wife. He didn't stay. He ran and ran until he stumbled to his knees, exhausted, crying and sobbing until sleep overtook him.

He had nothing to stay for. His known support of the rebel regime now made his death a certainty. He withdrew as many Syrian pounds as he could from the ATM, then set off in the clothes that he stood up in. He might have held a decent job in human resources, but that would count for little in other neighbouring countries. The only international commodity he could trade was a basic knowledge of the English language. If he was going to have to choose a country to rebuild his life, then it would have to be England.

It took several months trekking across Europe before he reached the channel. Then another three weeks before he found a lorry whose security he could breach. At last, he stepped out onto English soil in a service station he had never heard of on a road he had never travelled before.

Not wishing to be an illegal immigrant, Sobhy turned himself in to the authorities. He then spent the next four months in a detention centre awaiting the outcome of his application for asylum. Proving who he was, was bad enough, proving that if he was sent back to Syria, he would be in danger was even harder, when the government did not want him in the first place.

Luckily for Sobhy, in his mid-thirties, fit and reasonably attractive, his case worker had an instant preference for him, and they slept together on a number of occasions. Sobhy was just glad his case worker was a woman, although if it had been a man and it helped him to get his papers, then he would have done exactly the same.

Today, he had a national insurance number; he paid his taxes and had a steady income from his Uber driving. Although he would acknowledge he had achieved a great deal and overcome a mountain of hardships, he still could not erase the images of his daughter and wife, killed by his fellow Syrians.

"Are you sure this is the address you want sir?" Sobhy asked, having been instructed to park on the road outside a burnt-out house. If that was not bad enough, the two passengers were not average in the least. The younger of the two had a strong upper-class accent, the older one, well, he might have spoken a lowlier form of English, but he was dressed as a woman!

"Yes young man," the one in the dress told Sobhy. "Plus, I want you to wait for us; it'll only take fifteen minutes at the most. And yes, I know I pay waiting time. Come, Martin, let's get to it."

Sobhy's natural inquisitiveness wanted to ask the reason they wanted to enter this wreck of a house in the middle of the night. Afraid of what the answer might be, he kept quiet and patiently waited for their return.

***

With only the light from their paltry phone torches, Martin and Colin edged their way into the house, their feet crunching on the charcoal fragments that littered the floor. They first looked in the burnt-out living room. Colin shone the light around, stopped, examined a charred object before moving on to the next possible piece of evidence. Carefully he walked around the room. Martin remained static under the charred door frame; the rank odour of smoke still clinging to the walls.

Colin bent down and picked up a metal box, which had warped in the heat.

"Here's a clue, Martin." He appeared to be reading from the side of the box, difficult in the poor light and without his glasses. "Acme fire starting box, press red button and retire at least thirty yards before the box starts a raging inferno."

"Very funny."

"I thought so too." Colin laughed as he threw the box back on the floor. "Let's have a look at some other rooms."

They edged their way through the hallway towards what must have been the kitchen. It was nowhere near as burnt out as the living room, yet all the cabinets were covered with a layer of black soot from the smoke that must have filled the room. The units also looked to be damaged by the amount of water the fire brigade pumped into the house, the chipboard doors and worktops were bloated and distorted.

There seemed to be nothing that took Colin's fancy in the kitchen, except for his barbed comment that the design looked to be very old-fashioned, no doubt Rodney's mother had not changed the kitchen in years. The fact was borne out by the twin-tub washing machine located close to the sink, the once cream enamel sides were now cracked and rusted, stained with ash.

Carefully they manoeuvred up the stairs, which appeared to be reasonably intact. The paint on the banister had peeled off and the carpet was scorched. Fortunately, the wooden treads remained firm under their feet.

"Look at this," Colin pointed out, as he stepped into what was at one time a bedroom before the fire blackened the walls and the smoke tainted the bed sheets. "Almost in one piece. You see the way the back half of the house is relatively untouched by fire, just water and smoke damage in this part. The fire I think started in the living room, which was totally gutted."

"Was it the Acme fire box which proved a vital piece of evidence for you?"

"Don't be silly, just basic science, that's where the fire would have started. You told me earlier the insurance company thought it started in the living room."

"Now you believe them."

"I only believe what I can see and prove to myself; everyone else has an angle and a reason to see the truth through their eyes. They might have said the fire started in the living room, but they haven't worked out why it started. But for me, a real ex-detective, here is where the clues really are."

Colin pointed towards a dressing table, well more of a plain table with a freestanding mirror. The mixture of male deodorants and aftershaves pointed to the fact this might have been Rodney's bedroom. Colin picked up a torn photograph, then scrabbled around and found the other half. He then put the two parts together.

"A young couple, is this your Rodney?" Colin asked, as Martin shone his phone torch at the picture.

"Yes, and I think I recognise the woman he is embracing. I'm sure she is the dance teacher at the class where Imogen's husband spends his Sunday nights. Her name's Tracey. Fancy her being Rodney's girl."

"Really? Interesting." Colin put the photograph back on the table and continued to look around. It was not the only photograph that had been torn. The floor, once they looked more closely, appeared to be littered with fragments of photographs. There was also a photo album ripped to shreds. Colin went to the wardrobe, at the bottom was a pile of shirts and trousers, some partly torn, others pulled into ribbons of material.

"I might not know who started the fire yet, but I can see the motive for it, a broken relationship, we just need to find out who ended it and why."

Chapter 11

In the six years that Anne-Marie Marzec had worked at the Harby Hall Hotel she had never been asked such a question. She liked early morning starts, hence her permanent position as one of the three in the breakfast serving team. It also meant that once her shift was finished, she could binge on a big free breakfast, which would last her until her evening meal.

As an amiable waitress she was of course asked lots of questions by the diners: 'Is the bacon streaky?', 'Can I have my egg sunny side down?', 'How big are the sausages?' and her favourite, 'Can I have my tomatoes skinned?' One question that she had never been asked before was: 'Who is your local member of parliament?'. Today that odd question was added to the list of strange requests that would appear in her long planned, well overdue biography.

"Pardon?" Anne-Marie asked. She could have misheard the question or the old lady asking it might not have had her false teeth fixed correctly and have mispronounced a word. Although Anne-Marie was finding it hard to work out how you might verbally distort a breakfast item to make it sound like member of parliament.

The old lady huffed and begrudgingly repeated her question a little louder this time. "I said, who is your local member of parliament, assuming you live locally that is."

Anne-Marie hesitated, "I don't know."

"What do you mean you don't know?" Mother was not impressed.

"She means she cannot name her parliamentary representative," Martin interjected, to which his mother retorted sharply, "I know that. Please, I am able to deal with this matter without your help.

"Young lady are you telling me you have no idea who brings the voice of your constituency to the House of Commons. Well, I am staggered, what do the younger generation expect if they take little interest in the affairs of state?"

"Why should I know, they're all the same, you can't trust any of them; they're all in it to line their own pockets." Having had her say, Anne-Marie was keen to change the subject, so she asked, "What would madam like for her breakfast?"

"I suppose that is all the younger generation are good for, taking orders. I will have smoked haddock with an unbroken poached egg placed carefully on it. I do not want it alongside the haddock, is that clear? I want it on top of the fish."

Fortunately for Anne-Marie the remaining guests were a lot less troublesome. Martin asked for the full English breakfast. Susan wanted the same without that black pudding thing. Becky asked for just scrambled eggs on toast. Colin was the only one happy to collect his breakfast from the continental breakfast buffet, pointing out that he needed to look after his figure if he was going to wear the Dorothy Perkins dress he had his eye on.

When Anne-Marie returned to serve the breakfast meals to the Hayden table, Mother was quick to point out that the waitress's local MP was a gentleman by the name of Ignatius Fitzgerald, information that Anne-Marie could happily have lived without.

This gem of knowledge Mother now held was by virtue of Becky making use of her smartphone and Googling local MPs. This simple action deeply impressed Mother whose grasp of technology was very limited and understood even less. She compared what Becky did to having a pocket version of Debrett's in her handbag. Mother then made further use of Becky and the MP's Wikipedia page to see if he came from the same Fitzgerald family that lived in Lincolnshire and who Mother had known for years. The parents of Ignatius were indeed the Mr & Mrs Fitzgerald of Little Priory Farm, where Mother with her late husband had spent several high society weekends, the men shooting and the women gossiping.

As she finished the haddock that had been cooked and presented the way she preferred, Mother indicated to Martin that this detecting lark was not very hard, all you needed was a smartphone and Becky and you could find out most things. Martin ignored the barbed comment, opting to point out his own recall of the Fitzgeralds.

"Is this the same Mrs Fitzgerald who you once described as a pompous, self-centred bitch, who only sent out invitations to stay at Little Priory Farm to rub people's noses in the Fitzgerald wealth?"

"I did not use the 'B' word, I called her a self-centred mercenary. As for the wealth, that quickly drained away when her old man ran off with a woman twenty years his junior. I understand that she now has to open her gardens to tourists and sell cream teas at an exorbitant price to make ends meet."

"So it is the same Fitzgerald family that you once pledged never to cross their threshold again."

"Martin, you are being a snot. Sometimes one must swallow one's pride in order to achieve one's end. I will call on her for lunch today and get a personal meeting with her son, the MP. I am sure he will be able to take up the responsibility of getting the true recognition for Mrs Thatcher's birthplace."

The breakfast party watched with interest as Mother rummaged around her cavernous handbag. Finally, she pulled out a well-worn red leather address book, which she flicked through, until she found the page she was looking for. She returned the book to the hollows of her handbag. Again she searched, this time she pulled out an ancient mobile phone and then proceeded to dial the number she had located.

"Mother you do know…," as Martin started, he was immediately interrupted.

"Yes, I know I could transfer all my numbers to this phone and use something called speed dial. I once fell into that trap with a Palm Pilot many years ago. It worked fine until one day the damn thing gave up the ghost and everything was lost, including my contacts and more importantly, my diary. I now trust in a good old-fashioned pen and paper which has sufficed mankind for centuries."

"She has a valid point," Colin concluded. "If Moses had picked up the Ten Commandments from Mount Sinai, then got back home and the file was not compatible with his own operating system, well, that would have been embarrassing, as well as having severe consequences for civilisation."

Martin ignored the comment and Susan's laughter as he watched, much against her own regular advice to him, Mother made a telephone call from the table at a mealtime. It was an action that he urgently wanted to point out to his mother. He refrained however, knowing that she would make up some sort of excuse as to the urgency of the call that could hypothetically save humanity from suffering the indignity of Margaret Thatcher's birthplace remaining discreet.

The table remained silent as they listened with interest to Mother verbally smooch and snuggle up to Mrs Fitzgerald, pleading for a luncheon with her oldest and dearest friend as she was passing so close to her home. For whatever reason, the request was gracefully accepted and Mother had completed stage one of her master plan. She retired to her room with a smug smile.

"Martin, I didn't like to ask before," Susan started, "but now Mother has gone, why does your breath stink of last night's alcohol and your hair reek of smoke?"

"Oh Suzie Baby," Colin interrupted instantly, "I can answer that question with a lot more honesty than Martin will ever admit to."

"Well?"

"It's my fault that Martin stinks like an overflowing ash tray. Last night, heavily under the influence of drink, we visited the burnt-out house, and I came up with a perfect theory, hence it was a late finish. This morning, Martin couldn't get out of bed, he almost missed breakfast and there was no time for him to have a shower. Hung over, poor Martin just can't hack it, can you?"

"I would add," Martin said, "in my defence, Colin spends an inordinate amount of time in the bathroom, leaving me no choice but to arrive here, unusually for me, as one of the unwashed."

"Now that's taking one for the team," Becky praised the uncomfortable Martin.

"Thank you for your support, Becky. Rest assured I will be showering before we go out later to continue our investigations." Martin endured Susan's light-hearted attempts to fan the smoky odour away from her. "Apart from hogging the bathroom, Colin does not have any contacts in the police in this part of the country. But he has wisely suggested that we contact the local paper who might have some additional information about the fire."

Colin then continued the discussion explaining to those left at the table his theory about a relationship break-up being the root cause of the fire, that looked as though it had been started deliberately. He suggested that finding the girlfriend and speaking to her could be useful. In Colin's opinion, it was looking more and more likely that Rodney had started the fire himself, in line with the insurance company's theory.

As Becky and Susan left the table, Colin, taking his half-drunk coffee, moved around to occupy the empty seat next to Martin.

"I'm glad the girls have gone; I wanted a quiet word."

Discreetly, almost in a whisper, Colin began to explain that he had heard from Susan about the launderette and the groom's father, an odd story, based on rumour and conjecture. Martin spoke almost in support of Henry Phillips.

"That might be so," Colin told Martin in a tone that he normally reserved for important subjects, which made Martin pay particular attention to what he was saying. "But I have some serious concerns having seen something yesterday, although at that time I didn't know I was looking at Henry Phillips."

Martin listened carefully as Colin explained how he had seen, who he now knew to be Mr Phillips, ushering with a sense of urgency two women into a block of flats. He suggested visiting the women and finding out what they were up to in there.

"Makes a lot of sense. Susan and I will pop over later, it's not far and hopefully they will be in."

"Not a good idea, Martin. It's the reason I didn't mention this nugget of information within earshot of Susan. If, and only if, they are running some sort of brothel in the flat, then the appearance of a man and a woman is not the sort of visitor they would willingly open the door to, unless you have pre-arranged by phone a special session, if you get my drift. But if you turn up on the doorstep and ring the bell, well, a single man waiting to be let in is what they do, you're just a customer."

"And I do what?"

"Not what they expect; just ask some questions. The chances are, if they're running that sort of business from the flat, they'll just chuck you out, which is as incriminating as you can get."

"Keep a secret from Susan; are you sure?"

"She'll find out in the end, she always does. Then she'll rant and rave, but at least you would have found something out. And you never know where these things lead to. It could all be innocent, or you might find something else out. That's the fun of detecting; you can never tell where the leads take you."

Chapter 12

"What do you want?" The question was sharp without any type of pleasantry. If Mr Isaac Foxton, founder of the Grantham Gazette in 1878, had heard his receptionist speak that way to customers he would have sacked her on the spot. Fortunately for Gloria, Mr Foxton had been dead for many years so had never heard her customary greeting for anyone who walked into 'her' newspaper office.

The Grantham Gazette began printing news stories during the reign of Queen Victoria. In its heyday throughout the 1960s, it employed over twenty reporters and even more sales and administration staff. When the decline of local newspapers began, the Gazette was no exception. Today, it operated out of a small office just off the High Street, with an editor who also did the job of copy reader, sub editor, sports editor as well as letters reporter. There was another person employed as a reporter who was good, yet belligerent, and so allowed to focus on stories and not multi-task. The sales side of the paper was just one travelling salesman. Besides Gloria, there was an office worker who dealt with all the oddments of paperwork.

Gloria, who looked like she was forever sucking lemons, had been with the newspaper twenty-five years for the simple reason, whenever a round of redundancies were required, no one had the courage to tell her she was no longer needed.

"We'd like to speak to a reporter about the fire that occurred a little while ago in Branston Road?" Martin asked innocently, unaware of Gloria's reputation.

"Which Branston Road?" came the brusque reply.

"Is there more than one in Grantham?"

"How should I know, I'm not an A to Z map. What district is it in then?"

"I have no idea; I'm only here for the weekend?"

"A tourist. What's a local fire got to do with you?"

"I'm helping a friend with his insurance claim. In the same road is a Roman Empire church, you know togas and centurions, all worshiping Jupiter, that Branston Road." Martin hoped the additional information might make the identification of the district easier.

"Sounds like Harby Parish. You'll need to speak to Ken Wilson."

"Does he cover Harby Parish as part of his patch?" This time Martin tried to sound a little warmer, in the vain hope of melting the icy voice of this woman.

"He's our only reporter, he covers everything."

It was at this point Susan decided she should pop a few words into the banal conversation. Unfortunately, it was not going to be helpful.

"Then what was the point of asking us which district the story was in when it had to be him who covered it, unless they let you out in the daylight from time to time."

Gloria did not take kindly to that; her cold eyes bore into Susan.

"We have a lot of news agency stories."

Martin quickly butted into the discussion that was shaping into a confrontation.

"Can we speak to him, this Ken Wilson?"

"It's a free country. You'll find him in Ladbrokes, four doors down the High Street."

"Well, if he's on a story we can wait until he comes back." Not that Martin wanted to wait too long in this office with Gloria, who he felt might suck out his soul at any moment.

"Ladbrokes is where he is most of the time. He'll be squandering his wages on some lame horse he has never met, all the same it will still take his money. He calls it an intellectual challenge; I call it plain stupidity."

***

It was not hard to find Ladbrokes. As retail shops go, it was one of the more modern in the town. Inside, it was a far cry from the last betting shop Martin had entered when he put a bet on the Grand National for his mother, her only indulgence that year and only because a friend of a friend had a horse in the race which was guaranteed to win. Mother thought it worthwhile risking five pounds. That was seven years ago, the five pounds was never seen again, in the same way Mother never gambled again or listened to any of her friends who said they were 'in the know'.

It might not have had a wide shop front, but it went a long way back. Smart wooden floors, comfortable, red-padded chairs, small tables allowing the punters to peruse the form books. The left side of the shop was a bank of television screens, some showing live sports, some showing betting odds and others promoting offers to encourage clients to gamble.

It was not hard to find Ken Wilson in the betting shop. There were only a few other punters in the place and Gloria had given a detailed description of the reporter who they could see close to a slot machine, sitting on a high stool and leaning on a counter, making careful notations in a newspaper. Susan doubted it was the Grantham Gazette he was marking up.

With a discourteous voice, Gloria had described accurately the reporter as tall and lanky with a long, wrinkled, ugly face, who always wore a stupid flat cap even indoors and had a short blunt pencil tucked behind his ear which he never used. She added that even today, a warm day, Ken was wearing thick brown corduroy trousers and an over-washed, baggy, blue jumper.

Had Ken heard his description from the sharp-tongued Gloria, he would have said in his defence that the cap was there to cover his thinning grey hair, some wispy strands of which poked out from below the cap. The pencil was a habit. In previous years it had always been a cigarette tucked behind his ear, but having given up the unhealthy habit, his ear felt empty without something pushed behind it. A pencil seemed perfect for a reporter. As for clothes, it was all he had left that could be considered reasonably clean. Ever since his wife had decided he should do his own laundry, Ken had trouble getting to grips with a routine for doing his washing.

"Ken Wilson?" The question Susan asked caused the journalist to look up from his paper momentarily, then he returned to looking at the form for the two o'clock race at Lingfield. He spoke without looking at the two people standing beside him. Ken was not easily intimidated.

"Neither of you look as if you are at home in a betting shop. With that in mind, you are neutral in my view. Tell me, Proclaimer has won seven of his last eight starts at Kempton, is that going to be a better gamble than Totally Charming, who has placed over his last six races, even winning at this racecourse over a slightly shorter trip?"

Susan moved closer to him and looked over his shoulder at the open page of the Racing Post. Without rushing, she glanced down the list of runners, tutted almost silently, then stabbed her finger onto the paper.

"Amber Island, that's the one. Course and distance winner, recent win at Wolverhampton. If the going is good to soft, she'll walk it even with her handicap. At four to one, she must be worth a punt." Susan had given her verdict, which surprised Ken Wilson and shocked Martin, having never realised that she knew anything at all about horse racing. "Proclaimer might have won the last few of his races," she added, "never won at Lingfield, which has a shorter run to the line than Kempton, where you said he won the previous races."

Ken nodded in appreciation and respect; he marked out Amber Island for a ten-pound bet, he liked the girl's logic.

"Thanks. How did you find me?"

"The receptionist at your office seemed to think you would be here," Martin admitted, wondering if given Susan's confidence, he should put a few pounds on Amber Island himself. Then he recalled his mother's experience of gambling on horses.

"Gloria, she can be the biggest pain in the arse at times. Here I am trying to have a break from work and she's sending me people to talk to. I suppose you have a story which you think is earth-shattering."

"Given the detailed description she gave for you, I would say she has the hots for you," Susan pointed out, having seen the tell-tale sign of a woman fixated.

"Yes, she's obsessive as well as cruel and vindictive. She enjoys being a control freak who likes to get her own way and screw up my life as best she can. The woman is a first-class bitch."

"That's not a kind thing to say about your fellow employee," Susan stated, as she surveyed the runners in the two forty-five at Lingfield. Martin's Mayhem seemed a logical choice for a bet.

"It would be so much better if she was just my colleague, but sadly for me she is also my wife. And before you ask, I was very hung over, distracted, and broke when I agreed to marry her. However strange it might seem, apparently, they aren't valid reasons to have a marriage annulled, hence I am stuck with a bitter and twisted cow. That's enough of my hardships. What story do you want me to write about?"

Martin explained about the fire at Rodney's house and the allegation that the church used the power of prayer to combust the place. It was an old story, but Martin wanted to know as much as he could about what had happened and whether the newspaper had covered the story in any great depth.

Ken leaned back against the counter and pushed the rim of his cap further back, appearing to be settling himself for a long story. It turned out not to be that long.

He sounded bored as he explained house fires, unless there were any deaths, were not of interest to the paper. The fire itself he heard of the following day when he did his daily ring around of contacts to see what he had missed while he was in the betting shop. In fact, that day he recalled well, he was in Ladbrokes, having collected a useful fifty pounds from a rank outsider, Crimson Sand, an Irish horse that had not done much since. A house fire in Branston Road, no one hurt, was not of the slightest interest to him. Until, that is, about a week later Rodney telephoned suggesting that the church next door had caused the fire by the power of prayer. Ken's first thought was that if the church could burn a house down by prayer, they could, sure as hell, make a horse win its race, now that was his sort of church.

As the diligent reporter he was, he checked with the fire brigade, who confirmed that the fire had started in the front living room. There were traces of a small amount of accelerant, perhaps from a spilt bottle of white sprits, but certainly not gallons of flammable liquid sploshed around to start an intense inferno. All their information was passed onto the police. The local constable dug around a bit and couldn't put his finger on who, why, or what. Plus, with a nutter of an owner pleading that it was the Roman god Jupiter who did it, they put it to one side. It was not a priority for them. The fire brigade, tempted as they were to log it as a fireball from the hand of Jupiter, left it in their filing tray. The insurance company, as with all insurance companies, will happily take your money, yet when the time comes to pay a claim, was a little more reluctant. Picking on the possible presence of an accelerant, they decided they could not pay out.

Ken concluded, "Now Rodney is sitting in his caravan planning revenge on the deity, which is Jupiter, not a fair fight to my mind."

"What's your opinion?" Martin asked.

"Me, I don't really give a toss. Having met the man, he's not the full bus ticket, excuse the pun, he's a bus driver, if you didn't know. About the time of the fire, he was working late, so to my mind he doesn't look like the culprit. But I am damn sure it was not Jupiter who burnt his house down, either in person or commanding one of his weird disciples from the church next door."

"And what about the church next door? Do you have an opinion on them?"

"The way you two are speaking, I can tell you're not local. So let me ask you first, what's your interest in the fire and the church?"

Before Martin, who had been the lead in the conversation up to that point, could answer, Susan butted in.

"We're private investigators, who have an interest which we do not plan to share with you at this point. But we do value your thoughts on the church."

"Oh exciting. Better keep you two on my side, there might well be a story behind your secretive investigations. I'll paraphrase my thoughts. Dave Harvey, the church leader, is a known, if not proven villain. He's running the church. He is, without doubt, making money out of it and judging by his previous escapades, he will get away with it. Unless you two have other plans for him?"

"What about Henry Phillips, the butcher character? What's the gossip on him?" Again, Susan asked the question, to which Ken smiled and nodded his head.

"You two are busy little bees."

In his head, Ken was swirling around their questions. Obviously, they were new to the area, not fully aware of everything that was going on and were possibly adding things up incorrectly. First, there was the fire, with Rodney the bus driver, then questions about the church, which no doubt would be focusing their attention on Mr Harvey and now they wanted to know about Mr Phillips. In part, Ken could see where the conversation might be going, he knew all about the brothel above the launderette, which according to the shady Dave Harvey, was rented out to 'mister everyone's friend' 'butcher extraordinaire' Henry Phillips.

"I can imagine the concerns you might have about Mr Phillips. You've probably heard about the bloke and his string of butcher shops, plus some extra business interests, which is where all the gossip goes. I would advise you to speak to Henry Phillips privately and let him give his side of the launderette story. As neutral observers, I'd be interested to hear if you believe him or not."

***

It was no surprise to Susan that Rodney greeted them at the door of his caravan in the same clothes he had worn two days ago. Little Jupiter seemed pleased to see her again, no doubt hoping that she would take him away for another night in a luxurious hotel. Although Rodney did not look too impressed that she and Martin had turned up at his door, he invited them in, just no beers were offered today.

"Lucky to have caught me, off to work soon, doing a late today. About to take this little one for his walk before I go. Here, let me move those clothes off the chair so you can sit down. How did you get on with the church? Bunch of charlatans, aren't they?"

Martin began in a tone that was both firm and a little frustrated, "Rodney, tell us about your girlfriend, is she still around?"

Not wishing to answer at once, Rodney first unwrapped a Mars bar and took a large bite from it. Between chews, he answered, "Single man like me, lots of girls on the books, if you get my drift." He winked and wiped chocolate from the stubble around his mouth. Susan imagined that the only women he had on his books would be characters in them and not tangible at all.

"The girlfriend, who I am told, left you just before the fire," Martin persisted, as he stopped little Jupiter from jumping onto his lap.

"Ah, her. Good riddance to her, that's what I say. She was alright at first, then demanding. She was only after my money."

Well, that was his excuse. One of many he related around the circumstances of his lady friend deciding that she had had enough of him. Between a can of Red Bull and another Mars bar, Rodney told them the story.

They had been going out for a couple of months when she had suggested that the house and grounds now that his mother had died was just too large for him. He disagreed, saying it would not be right to sell the house, losing all the memories he had of growing up there and being with his mother. The girlfriend insisted that it would be good for both of them to make a fresh start, which did have its attractions for Rodney, but his loyalty to his mother's memory was still stronger. It was when his girlfriend said she had found the perfect buyer, the church next door. Although they wanted it mostly for the garden, they would be happy to buy the whole plot.

Rodney explained that he was a member of the church at the time, so the senator and others were already pushing him to sell. He did admit he was tempted, but said he wanted to wait another year, which did not go down too well with the church as they said they already had outline planning permission for the temple they wished to build and wanted to get started.

Rodney did not like the thought of being pushed into anything. The church decided that as he was left-handed, he was bad luck and they didn't want him at the church any longer. Then his girlfriend said that he was being stupid and petty. That was when they had their row, not their first, but it did turn out to be their last.

Whatever she said, Rodney no longer believed her and knew her true motive. She just wanted a pot full of cash to help her start a business and she wanted Rodney to shell out his money to help her. As if that was not enough, he had seen her with another man. When he was on nights, which in reality finished about midnight, he had seen her get out of a car. It was a posh car that he recognised belonged to Dave Harvey.

"I ask you, Dave Harvey, the overlord of the church, what does he have that I don't?"

At this point Susan was extremely tempted to suggest that maybe she could make a list of things that Dave had and Rodney did not, starting with hygiene. However, to use a phrase she had heard on the Rockford Files, Rodney was on a roll and singing like a bird.

Rodney continued with his saga. After his girlfriend had walked out, he realised he was going to face the wrath of the church and indeed he did, which culminated in his mother's house being burnt down. Now they knew he was living in a caravan while he fought for justice with the insurance company.

"Maybe we should have a word with your girlfriend. She might have something that we could use against the insurance company," Martin said, wondering just how truthful Rodney was being with them.

"There's no point, is there? She'll just bad mouth me, tell a bunch of lies and make me out to be a slob. A waste of your time."

Susan held her tongue and did not say that the girlfriend was right, he was a slob.

"Rodney, you forget we are detectives," Martin told him, partly to remind himself that he was an investigator. "I know your young lady is a dance teacher; it will not take much to find an address for her. You might as well tell it to me now to save all of us a lot of time."

Under his breath Rodney was muttering something as he wrote out the address of Tracey Johnson. Martin did not really care, he just wanted to get out of the caravan and get some fresh air.

***

"That was well impressive," Susan admitted, as they walked past the burnt-out house. She slipped her arm into Martin's. "How did you know the dance teacher was his girlfriend?"

"Easy really. As you know, last night Colin and I paid a visit to that derelict building," he pointed to the house they were walking past, "her photographs were in what looked to be Rodney's bedroom. I recognised her from the dance class we attended."

There was a look in Susan's eyes that Martin recognised. The look of a young mischievous girl who had just seen her next adventure. She was looking at the house with its blackened glassless windows and charred door frames. It was no surprise to him when she said, "Let's go in. I've never been in a house ravished by fire."

"It's ravaged by fire. Even so, we can't just walk in there; it still is Rodney's property."

"And last night it wasn't? Or should I get totally plastered and turn up here at midnight, then it will be alright."

"It wasn't the best decision I have ever made, but it simply does not seem right to walk in during daylight hours."

"Come on, I'm going in anyway. Follow me if you want." Susan broke free from Martin, hurried to the door and dived in.

"You need to be careful; it is dangerous in there." It was a feeble attempt at scaring her off, it failed and Martin found himself following her into the house, not that he really wanted to, but he was not going to see her do something silly and hurt herself.

The excitement level for Susan was on a par to opening Christmas presents as a child. She would be awake by four in the morning, drag her two bleary-eyed older sisters downstairs, and be ripping open presents in record time. The practice was put a stop to by their parents who missed out on the looks on their children's faces when they saw their gifts. It was also supported by the older sisters who preferred to remain asleep until a more suitable time.

Now, stepping carefully around the fire-damaged front room, she imagined she was a TV detective about to uncover a burnt body and a vital clue to the murderer. Some aromas walking around she had never experienced before. The smell of stale smoke, the acrid odours from the synthetic materials that had been destroyed, teased her every sense. Nothing had really prepared her for the total destruction of the room and the blackness of everything in it. With charred, unidentifiable objects cracking under her feet she moved into the hallway, and at Martin's direction, up the stairs.

Just as Martin had told her, the upstairs was relatively untouched. He showed her the bedroom and the photographs and the other evidence that Colin had pointed out.

"They do look an odd couple," Susan commented as she fanned through some of the torn photographs."

"Not that odd," Martin observed, "remember her grimy hands, peculiar for a dance teacher. Plus, what would she have seen in Rodney in the first place? We should have asked how they met."

"We'll ask Tracey when we see her, women on the whole are more romantic than you blokes. However they met, they must have liked each other then, if not at the end. I guess that's just the way of relationships."

"Some relationships must work," Martin suggested.

"Yes, but all the time you're hunting around for the perfect partner, there will be plenty left along the roadside. All those broken relationships, in the end you've got to wonder if it's all worth it. I'm getting a little fed up with searching for Mister Right if he even exists."

"That's a very defeatist attitude. I thought you were the fun-loving type?"

"There's only so much heartbreak and grief one can take in life. I've had my share of fickle men being bad-mouthed and the tears. All I am saying is that it's a lot of hard work trying to find the right man. When you think you have found him, he's nothing like you expected, or he shows no interest in you. Either way, grief and tears. Let's say me and men are paused for a while."

She turned away from Martin and started opening drawers and cupboards with their warped water-damaged doors. Then she noticed something discarded beside the wardrobe.

"Martin, these look like ladies' leggings."

He looked at the item of clothing she was holding up.

"Being here in daylight is a lot easier than groping around by the light of a phone torch," he admitted.

"And being sober helps as well," Susan teased. "The odd thing is, these are a size eighteen, therefore they're for a plump woman, something that the dance teacher is not."

"You sure they are not Rodney's?"

"I doubt it, if after being in a smoke-filled room, they still look cleaner than anything he might wear." She dropped them back on the floor, then continued her examination of the room. On each side of the double bed was a bedside cabinet, which consisted of little more than an open box. On the top of one was a Red Bull tin on its side, a bus magazine and a packet of toffees. Underneath in the hollow was a book. Susan took it out, flicking through the crinkled pages, stained yet still readable. The cover had no doubt got soaked as the firemen went about their business, now the edges were dried and frayed, the plastic covering peeled away.

"This is odd night-time reading for our friendly bus driver, 'Medieval Coins'. Maybe, as he's no longer a Roman, he fancied himself as a medieval citizen."

"Or he wanted to go into competition with Dave Harvey by opening a church from the Middle Ages," Martin added.

***

Standing on the pavement in front of Rodney's burnt-out house, Martin looked at his watch. Time was getting on and the questions they had asked had resulted in few answers and still more questions. This was not what he had planned.

Earlier at the hotel, he and Susan had checked out, then packed their luggage away in the boot of his car. What

Susan had not known was that he had provisionally booked two rooms for that night. His expectation was the investigation would take most of the day and then he would suggest that it would be better to stay for another night. Dinner together, chatting, smiling, laughing, enjoying themselves, nothing more. He was not planning to drag her to his room or anything like that. He just wanted to be alone with Susan a little longer.

It all seemed to be going to plan until Susan made her viewpoint about relationships and saying she was planning a hiatus on such emotions. That should not have worried Martin. She would after all still be the same amiable Susan, with the bizarre sense of humour and tilted view of life and those around her. It would have been no different to their everyday interactions. Now he knew she was not planning to seek a new boyfriend; he just did not understand why it should trouble him so much.

Maybe, because of her attitude, staying an extra couple of nights would be a waste. The situation had reached a point in the part of Martin's mind that was defeatist. He decided that he no longer cared who started the fire in the detached house behind him. He had little concern as to whether or not the insurance company ever paid out on Rodney's claim. As for the Roman church with its mind set in a time centuries ago, he was neither concerned as to how their money was made or where it went. He regretted Susan finding that dog and ever listening to Rodney's problems. His main concern now was getting back to his own bed tonight, in the relative calm of central London. More importantly, move away from the feelings he knew were rising inside him; being back home would curtail them instantly.

It was time to wrap things up. He knew doing such a thing was not going to please Susan. He knew that she would happily spend the next few months searching out the arsonist and delving into the procedures of the church. He needed a compromise which would keep her happy and get him out of Grantham by nightfall.

"Time's getting on Susan. I suggest that we split up, you go and speak to Tracey, I'll visit Henry, and we'll meet back at the hotel. We can see what we have, then probably go back to London."

"You might think of yourself as a detective Martin, but I think you might be pushing it believing I can sort this out by teatime."

"I'm not planning to resolve it. If the fire brigade, the local police and the local reporter have not reached a conclusion about the fire, then what hope do we have? As for Henry, almost the same applies. Then the church, everyone thinks they are up to no good, but have the locals done anything? No, because there is nothing to find out. I still think Dave Harvey is getting a bad press."

"And what if Miss Tiny Dancer tells me she set fire to the place hoping that Rodney would die in the inferno?"

"We tell the police then go home. Every scenario I play out in my mind takes me back tonight."

Martin could sense the huffing of frustration in Susan, although she did not protest as much as he had expected.

"Maybe you're right. It does seem we're on the outside here, treading ground that has been walked many times. I'll grab an Uber to visit the dance teacher, see what she has to say."

"And I'll speak to Henry Phillips. We'll meet back at the hotel later."

Agreeing they had a plan of sorts, Susan booked an Uber on her phone, while Martin did the gentlemanly thing and waited for it to arrive before making his way to see Henry Phillips.

Sobhy Khaled heard his phone beep, a possible fare from Branston Street. He knew the road, having only been there the night before when taking the weird couple of blokes to the burnt-out house. Things like that only happened once in a blue moon, he hoped.

Chapter 13

Colin might be a lot of things, but Martin could not deny he had good observation skills. When he told Martin about the two girls and Henry Phillips at the flat, he only gave him the name of the road, but plenty of details. Martin knew he was looking for a two-storey block of flats on the left-hand side as you made your way to the crossroads near the birthplace of Mrs Thatcher. The block of flats was beyond a post box close to where Colin had parked.

About fifty yards along the road, the block of flats was flanked by two oak trees. The door was deep brown, no doubt a wood stain. That was where Colin had seen Mr Phillips encouraging two young ladies into the door. He could not point to which flat of the twelve the girls might have been taken, but he did have a good idea. When he had returned from the abortive visit to Mrs Thatcher's birthplace with Mother, the flat on the first floor, on the right of the main door, which now had its windows open and no curtains, Colin said he would put his money on it being the flat where the girls were taken. That was good enough for Martin to walk through the main door. The entry system proved no barrier using a tip that Susan had proffered a while back. He walked up the carpeted stairs to the first floor and knocked on the door of the flat which overlooked the road. There was no reply.

"They're all out," a rasping voice echoed around the hallway. Martin turned to see the source of the statement; a man was standing at the open door of the flat opposite the one Martin was interested in.

"Will they be in later?" Martin asked.

The old man, holding his door open, wearing shorts and a dirty white t-shirt that was at least two sizes too small for him, laughed, showing off a less than perfect set of teeth. "You a punter then?"

Martin was not sure what the old man was getting at, but as he walked towards him and stood closer to the open door, the pungent smell of marijuana was unmistakable.

The old man with drooping eyes which glistened with non-emotional tears, was more than happy to talk about the two young women who were his new neighbours.

They had moved in yesterday; an older man had helped them. They had nothing in the way of furniture, just a couple of suitcases and a black plastic bag. Odd, the old man concluded, having watched everything via the distorting spy hole in his door. Two young girls, wearing tight jeans and low-cut tops, showing too much cleavage, frankly he would have described them as tarts, not that he knew precisely, but decent women from his era never dressed that way unless they were in the business. The tall older man with red hair left the flat very soon after they had arrived and then the girls were quiet all night. They left this morning about ten o'clock and had not come back since. Maybe they were out on the streets doing their dirty business. Martin was then instructed by this odd old man, that he should perhaps come back later if he was looking for a bit of stuff.

Martin was unashamedly offended by the inference that this short man was making, he was not in the market for buying a bit of skirt. The way the old man described the women after only seeing them once, especially as he had not even spoken to them, led Martin to suspect that the old man was not the most tolerant of neighbours.

He was however nosy and had described without doubt Henry Phillips and his red hair. The overwhelming smell of marijuana coming from the man and his flat, encouraged Martin to ask, "Have you been smoking dope?"

"Health reasons," came the old man's defence. He lifted his hands up, so they were in Martin's vision. Martin could not miss the gnarled and swollen joints that plagued the old man's hands. "These things cause me a great deal of pain, so I smoke weed to help me through."

"I never knew the NHS provided such drugs," Martin said. In all honesty, he was unaware of what it provided in most areas of life. Unless you were run over or dropped down with a heart attack, he could not think why the NHS might help you with illegal drugs.

"Don't be so bloody daft! The health service doing something that helps the patient and not the politicians! I have to buy my own weed from a dealer. Costs a bit, but it's worth it to miss out on the pain from these painful hands."

Martin had to be honest, he had not met many people from the region, but there did appear to be a trend towards having a thing about smoking weed. He had assumed that any drug problems were confined to London, obviously he was wrong. What he did wonder was just where the old man might be buying his drugs. When he asked, the old man was not shy about his source, in his eyes he was not doing anything that might get him arrested. In fact, he sounded almost proud, as he described to Martin the supply chain he used.

"Well, it's all a little underhand, as I'm sure you can imagine, still, can't get it from the local corner shop, can I? But if you're interested, as you're the sort of bloke who seeks out prostitutes, then I can see no harm in mentioning that I get my supply from a gang called BPB."

Martin recalled that it was the same name as on the card Vera had given to him. This gang seemed to have a stronghold on the Grantham supply of weed.

"How do I get myself some?" Martin asked, not really understanding why having come to the flats to see what Henry Phillips was up to, he was now making enquiries about buying weed. It might open a can of worms, but something inside told him he was moving in the right direction. He still planned to leave Grantham tonight, even if that meant ignoring the worms he found in the tin.

From the pocket of his stained shorts, the old man pulled out a mobile phone, which looked a lot higher tech than any Martin had ever owned in his life. The old man flicked through some messages, before nodding.

"They change the rendezvous point daily, shrewd lot. Today, jump on the 160-loop bus, you can pick it up from the bottom of the road here. Watch out for a lady with purple hair, she'll be on the bus. Sit next to her and hand over twenty quid, you'll get a packet of goodies and then you can get off the bus. It's really that easy. Best not to mention my name, not sure how they'll take to free advertising. The bus does a circular route, so if you miss it, it will come back past again."

"Is that it?"

"Well, let's just say, it's a lot easier to buy dope in this town than get a decent loaf of bread. Let me know how much the girls charge, might save my pennies up, never done a duo before. Might be fun and help with the pain." Once again, he held up his knuckles to show Martin how deformed they were, this time, laughing. Martin was not impressed; in fact, he was a little disgusted that this man could only find solace for his pain in privately sourced drugs as the NHS could do little to help, but that discussion was for another day.

As Martin walked down the stairs he wondered if getting on a 160-loop bus might be worthwhile, he decided it might. So far, the weekend, apart from a boring wedding, revolved around prostitution, drugs and gods that burnt down houses. It was turning out to be very much expect the unexpected.

***

The bus stop was a few doors down from Margaret Thatcher's birthplace. Martin almost missed the small sign, wedged up close to a scout hall which was once a Methodist church. There was a plaque built into the side of the hall, that described the building as 'Primitive Methodist 1886', a term he had never heard of. The distraction caused him to swing around, realising that a bus was pulling away from the stop. Luckily it was the number fourteen, but he needed to pay attention to the buses stopping. He waited.

Martin recalled the last time he was on a bus. It was a double decker red bus, he was a teenager, and his father sat beside him. In his wisdom, he had decided it would be a good experience for his son to ride on public transport to overcome the natural aversion Martin had for it. They were going to Regent Street to purchase a new pair of shoes for him. The bribe had worked; an uncomfortable Martin joined the other people on a bus. He never did it again. Apart from the other passengers, none of whom he knew, he had to take part in the bizarre ritual of waiting beside a concrete pole that defined the stop and informed you of which buses were going to arrive. He then needed to be aware of where he was going, so he could select the correct bus. Once on, he had to constantly observe where he was to ensure that he could get off at the correct stop. It would have been all very well if he was making the trip every day, but the first time the stress levels were not worth the savings he might make compared to a taxi.

Taxis were in Martin's mind public transport, but there was never much waiting. In London, just stand by the road, raise your hand and a black cab will appear as if by magic. You tell them where you want to go, and they take you there while you sit back and relax. When you arrive, the cabby informs you. Everything about the journey is easy and free of stress. That was why Martin had not been on a bus in decades and as he stood patiently beside the concrete bus stop, he began to wonder how much they might have changed. For a start they were not red out here in the market town. He wondered what else might be different. His only consolation was the 160, he had been told, was a circular route. At least he might end up back here, close to where he had parked his car.

The 160 was a single decker bus, painted in a livery of pale blue and white, with a broad orange stripe between the two colours. There would be an enthusiast at the bus station who could have told you that it was a Dennis Dart ALX200. To Martin it was still a bus and very public. It stopped beside him and the door opened with a gushing hydraulic sound.

If Martin was apprehensive as he stepped onto the bus, then the driver was terrified when he saw him. The colour drained from Rodney's face as Martin stood beside the ticket machine, brandishing a credit card.

"How do I pay?" Martin smiled. All things in Grantham seemed to be joined in some way or other.

"What do you want?" Rodney asked.

"A bus ticket so I can ride on your bus; I think that's how these things work."

"I just drive around in a big circle; you'd be better off getting a cab."

Generally, Martin would agree. He would have chosen the cab over the bus, for the reasons that he had already reminded himself of. But this bus trip, he now hoped, would explain a little more about what was going on in Rodney's life, and the look on the bus driver's face told Martin that he was touching a raw nerve.

"Sorry, this bus has broken down, electrical failure. Best get off and wait for another."

At this juncture, Martin was a little concerned as he had to agree with Rodney, that the motor of the bus was not running, it was as silent as it had been since it arrived at the stop. The buses, or bus he had travelled on years ago droned on and on whilst passengers alighted and boarded. But that was back in the days of diesel and Martin recalled that even his own Honda had a system that stopped the engine when stationary and fired back into life as he depressed the clutch. Something to do with saving the planet.

"Doesn't it always do that?" Martin was starting to be the shrewd investigator he never knew he could be.

Not to be deterred, Rodney took drastic action by calling down the length of the bus informing the passengers that the bus had broken down. He blamed an electrical fault and stated he had already informed the garage who would send out a replacement, but if not, the number fourteen bus would take them into the town centre.

The announcement was met with resignation from the passengers, who knew you could never assume public service vehicles being on time, and you could guarantee some would be cancelled.

"Off you get Martin, sorry about this."

Martin stood on the pavement as the passengers trooped off the bus and gathered around the scout building, awaiting the next bus which they hoped would arrive without too much delay. Once the single door was clear of exiting passengers, Martin entered the bus once again, only to be told that the bus was going nowhere and he should not be on it.

"I'm a bit concerned about the little old lady at the back of the bus," he pointed towards a woman, "the one with the purple hair."

Ignoring Rodney's protests, Martin walked through the bus and settled himself beside the lady who looked at him with a smile.

"Well, it's the gum shoe! What you after, bit of nooky or something to smoke?" Vera asked.

Chapter 14

The address Rodney had given to Susan led her to Celtic Chapters, a small lock-up shop amongst a parade of other miscellaneous ones on a drained and ageing estate. She guessed the estate was once owned by the council, to use the modern parlance, for social housing. However you might wish to categorise the area, it was pleasant, calm, not much in the way of graffiti and Susan imagined it to be a friendly place to live. A location where neighbours talked to each other, and shoppers stopped to chat as they went about their chores.

Rodney had been precise with his directions. The girlfriend lived above the shop, which could be accessed through the single door to the left with a large number fourteen written on it. Susan rang the doorbell and waited.

"Can I help you?" It was the dance teacher. Susan recognised her at once, leaning out from the shop doorway. Equally Tracey remembered Susan from the most recent dance lesson she had overseen, the newcomer with her dishy partner.

Although Rodney had been clear and insistent about Tracey living above the shop, he had failed to mention that she was the owner. Susan assumed that oversight had been out of spite, not ignorance. Once she explained that she wanted to talk about Rodney and his fire, she was warmly invited into the shop to continue the conversation.

Celtic Chapters was not exclusively Celtic. Tracey also used the shop premises to promote her dance classes and to sell items that would help budding dancers become better.

The shop had a single door in the centre, with a chime that greeted customers. On each side of the doorway, there was a glass display window. The one to the left contained small display dummies that wore Celtic jewellery: wristbands, rings, ornate belts, headbands. Some were adorned with coloured glass stones, enamelled sections or even bright vibrant feathers. The display on the other side of the door was far from Celtic, but contained ballet shoes, leggings, tutus, everything a young wannabe ballerina could wish for.

Inside the shop was bursting with amulets, bracelets, clothing and the remnants of incense hung in the air, giving an ethereal feel to it. Magical was how Susan would have described it. A fairy-tale grotto. She could not resist the temptation of trying on wristbands as she conversed with Tracey.

"I was hoping you had come to book some more dance lessons. I could see that you both have a natural talent and fitted so well in each other's arms."

"I'm not local, so a little bit impractical, unfortunately. As I mentioned I just want to ask you a few questions about your ex-boyfriend, Rodney."

The two women sat down at the counter on high stools, facing each other, as if they were friends who had just met up for a coffee.

"Ask me some questions? Sounds like the police." Her voice was warm and light, with a hint of amusement.

"No, nothing like that. Private detectives looking to see how true his allegation is about the god Jupiter starting the fire."

"That must mean you are either working for the insurance company or Jupiter himself." Tracey laughed at her own joke, then pointed to the bracelet that Susan was still fiddling with. "Have that as a welcome gift, it suits you."

Marginally uncomfortable, a rare thing for Susan, she quickly put the bracelet on to the counter.

"Thank you, but I couldn't. Do you make all this stuff yourself?"

Encouraged by her question, Tracey proudly began a brief outline as to how she arrived in Grantham, owning a shop and running dance classes.

She was not especially interested in ornaments, Celtic or otherwise. Her real passion was working plain metal into useful objects. It was a love that began when she was a small child in her father's workshop. She was brought up in a small village outside of Sleaford. Her father was the local blacksmith, as were his forefathers. With fewer horses to shoe, Tracey's father shaped metal into wrought iron gates, floors for trailers, welding patches on the side of tractors and repairing car floors. Anything in metal he could craft and shape to fit almost any purpose.

As a young girl, Tracey would help her father operating the bellows that made the coals turn white, moving metal around the workshop, spraying the wrought iron, as well as listening to his stories of great past projects he had completed against the odds.

By the time she was a teenager, Tracey was an accomplished anglesmith, skilled at hardening and annealing. She could pour molten metal into a cast and use a die to press shapes out of metal plate. Yet even though she had acquired all these essentially masculine tasks, like her father she loved dancing. Both skills she now used to good effect to earn a living.

Wednesday afternoons and Sunday evenings, when her shop was closed, she offered dance lessons. The Wednesday sessions were more tea dances for senior citizens. Sunday nights, young at heart couples acted on her advice to move around the dance floor as if they were on a cushion of air.

"To make a living, I figured that creating Celtic ornaments, charms and trinkets would pay better than the heavy work of bending iron." Tracey then asked her earlier question again. "So, are you working for the insurance company?"

"To be honest, we, that is myself and my partner Martin, came up from London for a wedding. Fate brought us into contact with Rodney and his predicament about the insurance company not paying out."

"Interfering do-gooders."

Susan thought that was an odd thing to say, almost taunting, but chose to ignore it, maybe it was just a local harmless phrase. "Yes, you could say that, or I'd rather say do-gooders who care for others. Rodney seems to think that you wanted him to sell his house to the Roman church, to then skim some money off for yourself and shore up your business."

"I'm surprised he could put together so many thoughts in one conversation."

"Even so he seems to put a lot of the blame onto you. When you weren't going to get any money, you walked out."

"Oh, I walked out on him alright, but it wasn't over money. His interest in my money was at the beginning of our relationship. Let me explain." Tracey folded her arms and began to share the story of the liaison, to a very interested Susan.

Money had played a key part of her relationship with Rodney, not that she ever imagined when she first met him that he would be asking for money. But after his mother died, he had lost not only his last parent, but more importantly to Rodney, her pension. It was a large pension from her long career in the National Health Service. Overnight he had no one to cook for him or supplement his own meagre income.

He now had to pay all the bills plus cook for himself. Not the sort of activities Rodney had ever excelled at. When Tracey first met him, she felt sympathetic after his mother's death, and was prepared to help out with the financials, picking up the council tax charge, clearing the overdue gas bill for him. Also for some reason cooking for him, often after a late shift. Looking back, she had no idea just why she doted on him and pandered to his every whim, maybe she had looked upon him as a little child who needed protecting. However blinkered she was then, she continued to help him financially and offer advice. That guidance from the very start was to sell the house, he could never afford it with his job, even with all the overtime, the place was just too big and costly.

Rodney, being the dreamer he was, decided that he could keep the house and become an entrepreneur by renting caravans to holidaymakers in Skegness. He would start off with one unit, then the profits from that would let him secure another during the same year. He concluded that within five years he would have a self-generating fleet of caravans making him money, all for sitting around the house.

Well, it was a business plan, but he needed the money to start. Tracey paid for the caravan that was going to be the first in his fleet, the one he was now living in. At the same time, she bought the caravan with her hard-earned cash, the Roman church asked to buy a strip of land at the back of his house. He was interested, thinking it would buy him a second and third caravan. There was no mention of paying Tracey back. She pointed out that if he sold the land to the church, when he wanted to sell his house, the presence of a temple dedicated to Jupiter in his back garden, was going to greatly devalue his property. She suggested selling everything, land, garden, house, the whole lot. He could then invest more in his business as well as buy a smaller place to live.

"Whatever got into him I have no idea. Flying off the handle saying I'm working for them, doing their bidding. All sorts of wild allegations. Well, it was up to him, I didn't care. Then to make matters worse, he, having been a fully qualified toga wearer in the church, lost his place in the congregation. He put it down to the fact he wasn't selling his house to Dave Harvey.

"That's the money side of things for you. Not quite how he portrayed it, I daresay. As for breaking up, I did walk out on him, and I imagine you would have done the same thing, but it was not just about the money."

Tracey recounted that Rodney was not selling the house, had lost his place in the church and thought she was some sort of spy for them. All the while, the caravan was stuck in his garden while he was waiting for some vague mate to transport it up to Skegness. Things were now tense between them, Tracey readily admitted. Things got worse when she popped round to his house to prepare a slow cooker meal for his return after doing a long split-shift.

The first thing out of place was his moped still sitting by the back door. Maybe he had not gone in Tracey thought. Next there was an empty wine bottle on the table, a half-drunk bottle of vodka, also, there was a distinct odour of cannabis hanging in the kitchen air.

Without any hesitation Tracey ran up the stairs into Rodney's bedroom. It was no surprise to find him in bed with another woman, giggling and laughing together. Both of them were happy to ask, upon Tracey's arrival, if she would like to join them. That was never going to happen in a month of Sundays, Tracey confirmed. The worst thing about finding her boyfriend in bed with another woman was the woman herself, or a better description would be a pensioner.

A plump old woman with bright red hair who introduced herself to Tracey as Vera. Rodney explained that she was an environmentalist, which he seemed to think was some sort of excuse for being in bed with her.

Tracey called Rodney a 'first-class bastard', threw the nearest thing that came to hand at him, a can of Lynx body spray, then stormed out. Her love for him, if she had any, had died.

"Rodney seemed to imply," Susan pointed out, having enjoyed a saga that made her own love life seem mundane, "that you were connected to Dave Harvey romantically and taking his side over the sale of the house."

"Everyone knows Dave Harvey. I know him from dance classes that he took a couple of years ago. He still gives me a lift from time to time, he worries about me being on the streets late at night. There's nothing in it, honestly, just two friends. Rodney did blow the friendship up into a mass conspiracy against him. But that's Rodney for you."

"So after the episode with the pensioner, you never saw him again?"

"My dear, this is a small place, I see him from time to time, on and off his bus. I just avoid speaking to him. The last time we spoke was when I went back to collect some of my stuff. He was contrite, apologetic, not exactly grovelling but almost on his knees. I did feel sorry for him, I'm sad to say. But you're a woman, once you've been betrayed, there's no going back, is there?"

Yes, Susan knew exactly what Tracey was talking about, her plumber boyfriend had betrayed her in a similar way. Thankfully for her ego he had bedded a woman of her age not a red-headed pensioner. In fact, most of Susan's ex-boyfriends had turned out to be unreliable in one way or another. Being the optimist that she was, Susan was sure there must be at least one man out there who could be trusted and was trustworthy.

"How did the wedding go? Would I be right in suspecting it might have been Henry Phillips's son getting married?"

Susan confirmed it was indeed, and asked if it was the social event of Grantham's year, as everyone seemed to know about it.

"I wouldn't say it was as grand as that, but he does have a large dubious reputation in the town. He has this big shadow hanging over him, running a brothel, only rumours, nothing proved, but as they say, there's no smoke without fire."

"But you're a friend of Dave Harvey and there seems to be two very distinct camps of opinion as to who might have been running the brothel. Henry points the finger at Dave and Dave points the finger back at Henry."

"You've spoken to Dave?"

Susan nodded. Tracey seemed surprised that she had talked to him, let alone discussed the saga of the launderette. "Well, it could turn out to be more of a testosterone fight between the two of them. Tit for tat, you know how boys can be. Henry Phillips got a little vindictive and pulled some strings which as good as blocked Dave's chance of ever building his beloved temple."

"Even less reason for Jupiter and his followers burning down the house?"

Tracey nodded. "Maybe, although they do say God works in mysterious ways, I guess that can equally apply to Roman immortals."

***

"Is the purple hair some sort of disguise? If it is, it's not working."

"Well if you know me, you know me, I wear it this colour at work and red when I am being social. What brings you onto the bus if not for nooky or weed?"

"I heard the BPB were selling drugs on a bus. It seemed too weird to be true, but now it would seem that it is. How come you are selling drugs to Grantham residents?"

Vera was not shy in explaining her reasons to Martin. She was not excessively proud of what she was doing, neither did she feel guilty. To her it was a social service. Having worked all her life in a local food factory, being paid the legal minimum wage, she had no money left at the end of the working week to add to a pension pot. If she had put some away, then her kids would have gone without food, and she was not going to let them starve just so that she could live comfortably in her old age.

Now, alone in life, with just the state pension to keep her, barely enough to live on if she was frugal with her food and clothes. Well, she had done that all her life, she wanted more now she was a pensioner. Her dealing was the perfect way to supplement her retirement income and enable her to have those little extras that make life worth living.

She was also pleased and proud of herself for seeing a niche in the drug dealing market. There are, as everyone knows, the mainstream dealers, selling all types of hard drugs on the streets and using violence and threats to hang onto their patches. Vera had seen another market and another venue.

Her age group was the hippie drugs generation, free love and soft hallucinogenic potions. All of them were now pensioners and even if they fancied a little recreational drug-taking, did not feel safe to venture onto the streets and interact with hardnosed dealers.

Hence she started BPB, the Bus Pass Brokers. Supplying marijuana to the older generation, who used it for not just getting high, it also helped with the aches and pains of getting old. Plus, she could ensure that her prices were kept low and affordable for pensioners across Grantham.

"Why," Martin asked, "do you sell from a bus, isn't that a little risky?"

Vera laughed. "Not as risky as selling drugs on the patch of someone who is not averse to using a knife or a gun. Plus, buses are warm and dry. Standing on corners dealing I would feel the cold and the damp, which isn't good for my joints."

"What about CCTV?" Martin pointed to the darkened glass dome that kept watch on the passengers.

"I do my runs twice a week. Rodney, bless his little cotton socks, disables the cameras for me. I tell my clients which bus I plan to be on and they get to use their bus passes, hence our name. All very civilised and frankly, I think I am performing a service for an ageing population."

It all sounded very cosy and sweet. Even though Martin knew that Vera was breaking the law, after seeing the old man and his twisted hand joints, he could sympathise with her point of view.

"I heard that Rodney lost his place in the Roman church because he was selling drugs. Is he a competitor or an associate?"

Vera conceded that he was more of an associate. The problem with Rodney, she admitted, was that he had dreams beyond his ability to make reality. He wanted to become a millionaire through drug dealing. Well, even Vera could see that was never going to happen selling weed from the back of a bus. He tried selling some stock at his church and was quickly caught and thrown out. But he meant well and by helping Vera with her sales, he also got a generous cut and other perks of the job.

Martin did not want to think what the other perks might include and avoided that line of conversation.

"They might have thrown him out of the church, but would they deliberately burn down his house?"

"You sure you don't want to try a spliff?" Vera asked, as she rolled herself a joint and lit it, inhaling the smoke deep into her lungs. "It will help calm you down, you do seem tense at times. Are you going to turn me in?"

"I would say it would be a waste of time and a disservice to the elderly of Grantham, so I'll keep your activities to myself."

"He's really quite simple." Vera used her smouldering joint to point towards Rodney at the front of the bus, fussing and answering questions from stranded passengers. "Knowing what I was doing at the back of his bus I bet he panicked when he saw you get on. He should have remained calm; I keep telling him the police are not interested in people like me selling soft drugs. If we get caught, he can deny knowing what I was doing. But he has always been a mummy's boy doing her bidding and never having to decide for himself."

"As I understand it, the insurance company was going to pay out on his house until he told everyone the God Jupiter set it alight. Do you know why he changed his mind?"

"I'm not his mother you know. I don't understand why he changed his mind and frankly don't care, that's his problem. And before you ask, I never questioned him because I don't care about his personal life."

Chapter 15

In the end, Martin to his utter relief, did not need to ride on the bus. Vera told him all he needed to know. Rodney was the wild dreamer everyone said he was. After being thrown out by the church for selling drugs, he now acted as the facilitator for Vera to sell her weed to the pensioners of Grantham.

It was becoming increasingly clear that Rodney did not live in the real world. And although it was true his house had burnt down, Martin would not have put it past Rodney to have started the fire just so that he could then accuse the church of the crime. Of course, Martin recalled that Rodney was working on lates at the time, but he had breaks, he had a moped, and that gave him opportunity. It was not impossible to construct the theory that Rodney popped back, set light to the house and then returned to his work. The only thing that bugged Martin, was why Rodney did not accuse the church first of all. That was a barb in the side of his theory.

Yet that was for someone else to figure out, if anyone had the interest or enthusiasm to ask the question. For now, Martin just wanted to confront Henry Phillips, ask him to his face about the brothel above the launderette. It was something that he was not going to shy away from, the reporter and Edwin had said, 'ask Henry yourself.' They did not try and defend him in any way, which Martin had found odd. It was back to his car to take the short drive across town to the headquarters of Phillips Fillets.

It was not as ostentatious as Martin had expected. Located on a modern trading estate, Henry's company occupied two large units. The one on the left was a two-storey building, with big windows and a modern painted sign, making it clear who occupied it. Next door on the right was little more than a large metal box which overshadowed the offices, two articulated lorries were backed up to it. They were both sign-written with the livery of Phillips Fillets. Martin assumed that would provide a storage facility. It was nothing like an abattoir, possibly just a refrigerated holding area for the joints of meat that were transported across the country to shops, restaurants and hotels. Henry's business had expanded way beyond a few high street butchers.

Martin knew he was taking a chance just turning up in the hope that Henry would be there. If not, he reasoned they would at least know his whereabouts, which would then enable him to meet up with the groom's father. As luck would have it Henry Phillips was in his office, with a defence in the shape of a thin woman in her late sixties, with long stiff grey hair that she held back with a single plain elastic band taken from the stationery cupboard.

"There must be a reason for you wanting to speak to Mr Phillips," was her first line of protection for her boss.

"It's a personal matter following the wedding of his son, at which I was an invited guest." Martin wanted to sound stern and firm, although he would be the first to recognise that he did make it appear as if there was a number of uninvited guests at the soiree.

To her surprise, when she called Mr Phillips to inform him that a Mr Hayden was here without an appointment – a cutting remark on her behalf – Henry at once welcomed Martin into his office.

The two men shook hands firmly and Martin was ushered to one of four comfortable casual chairs in a corner of the large office, which were no doubt placed there for informal meetings. After he had refused the offer of a drink, Henry asked him the purpose of his unexpected visit.

The office might have been spacious in recognition that it belonged to the Managing Director and founder of the company, yet it felt cluttered. The walls were adorned with framed photographs, in the main of Henry shaking hands with a celebrity of sorts. Martin identified a couple of prime ministers and a number of government ministers. He even, to his surprise, recognised two semi-famous television personalities, whom he had read about, one of which he was sure was currently under investigation for sexual harassment. Although such an allegation did not seem to warrant exclusion from the Henry Phillips Hall of Fame.

A large desk placed in front of the panoramic window, was awash with papers and files, no doubt the working hub for Henry. Alongside the desk, to the left was a large cabinet filled with silver trophies and wooden awards and plaques, proclaiming the virtues and superb taste of Henry's meats. For all the pomp and circumstance of the room, Martin still needed to ask difficult questions.

It was not going to be easy to ask the father of one of your friends if he was running a number of brothels around Grantham. Martin disliked confrontation at the best of times, although having worked with Susan over a period of time, being dragged into situations that he had never experienced before had prepared him better for times like this. Martin had a plan.

"I have heard that your wife works in the local planning office and you are locally known for helping smooth things through that department. I am concerned that you are not sticking fully to the rules."

"Ah, a legitimate concern, one that I have been asked many times, as I make no secret of the fact that my good wife does indeed work in the planning department. I have nothing to hide. As I recall, your father owned a large business, I am sure he was an expert in his product, as I am an expert in cuts of meat. In fact, most business people are experts in their chosen field.

"Running any company needs a range of skills that we might not have, that is why we employ accountants, tradesmen, and take advice where we can. So, when someone needs to apply for planning permission, they come to me to ask questions, which I then ask my wife who advises. This enables the planning procedure to run smoothly and, in most cases, successfully. I should point out that there are several planning officers, so my wife ensures that she is never the officer responsible for my friends' requests. Does that address your concerns?"

If Martin was being honest, it did not totally quell his concerns, not that planning permission was his main interest, running brothels was his big question.

"It does sound a very cosy arrangement. Apart from prestige, what do you get out of it?"

"I like to help commerce in the town. It provides jobs for local people and boosts an economy, that in turn helps everyone, including me by selling more cuts of meat."

"I have heard that as a thank you, those that you help, who have a flat above a shop, allow you to rent it for about a year at a very good rate."

"I don't think that's a regular arrangement, or a price that needs to be paid for my assistance. It's just mutual aid between tradesmen. A bit like me providing meat at cost price to a restaurant as a favour to a friend."

Martin was sure that his mentioning of flats above shops had alerted Henry to the real reason for his visit. He sensed a concern in Henry's voice as he tried to answer the question in a vague manner rather than answering directly. He would make a good MP.

"And what interest would you have in renting a flat?"

"I cannot see how that would concern you in the slightest. You were worried about planning permissions; I have answered that question. What I do with rented property of any description should not really worry you. What I do is legal, I just don't like to talk about it much. There, does that satisfy your curiosity?"

"I have been told one of those flats you rented was a massage parlour and brothel with two young ladies. Don't you ever check your tenants?"

"Ah, now we have arrived at the true reason for your visit here today, haven't we Martin? Let me guess how you have arrived at my office wanting answers to some questions that have developed in your investigative mind. You are looking into the works of that colony of Romans based in Grantham. You have been speaking to Dave Harvey, who has told you about the launderette scandal. As I said, everything I do is legal and above board, you can either take my word for it, or you can take Dave Harvey's devious words as the truth. I hope you will take my word."

"In this instance, I do add more weight to what Mr Harvey has said, partly because the launderette scandal as you so put it, was confirmed by a local reporter who seemed to have an independent viewpoint on the whole situation."

It was a broad unexpected smile that broke across Henry's face. Martin ignored it; Henry could be throwing a dummy.

"Martin, I know you became a detective to avoid any real work because Howard informed me. A good wheeze indeed. I didn't expect to be sitting here answering questions following what appears to be a comprehensive investigation on your behalf. I must congratulate you, can't call you a faux detective anymore, can we?"

"Do you run brothels around Grantham?" It was the question Martin had wanted to ask from the moment he walked into the office. It was time to get to the crux of the matter.

"Okay, I think it's time for you to learn the truth, the whole truth, and nothing but the truth, for no better reason than as a good friend of my son's, I trust you. I am sure you are an honourable person who knows how to keep a secret, which is what my flats are all about. Of course, once I have told you, I cannot be sure you will believe me, yet if you do, I hope that you will maintain the discretion others have kept."

The first thing that Henry readily admitted to was the massage parlour above the launderette owned by Dave Harvey. Yes, he had rented the flat and had installed two women, neither of whom knew each other before they began sharing.

Unfortunately, he did not know what they were up to until he was told about their activities from others. At once he removed them from the flat and sent them to the local council so that they could deal with their housing crisis.

"To understand the whole picture, you need to hear about another side of my family's life and the real reason I have a number of rented flats around the area."

Martin was sceptical as Henry began his explanation. He started with the little-known fact of his daughter's work. She was now in her late thirties and worked for a charity, one that she and a friend she met at university started together. They supported women, who were victims of domestic violence, in any way they could, ensuring court orders were taken out against the perpetrators and in rare circumstances, rehousing the victim to ensure their safety, normally through the local council where they lived. There were occasions when circumstances and locality were against the victim and housing needed to be found quickly as far away from the perpetrator as possible. That was where Henry said he got involved with helping the charity.

"Through my many contacts and by smoothing the planning applications for friends, I have access to accommodation, like the flat over the launderette for example. We install the very often young women, although age is no respecter of domestic violence, into the flat. They're in an area they have never been to before, no friends, nothing but a suitcase full of treasured belongings.

"We put them into a furnished flat, sharing with another victim for support hopefully. I, again through my contacts, ensure they get paid work in one of the many food manufacturing plants that frequent the countryside in south Lincolnshire.

"As I mentioned, I get the flat either free for the year or at least a very competitive rate, which my company is able to cover. For a year the women have work, no bills to pay and time to rebuild their lives. In almost all cases, they move on and settle in a new safe life, either here in Grantham or further afield. The system works well and there is no permanent place where the women live, the work of the charity can be very discreet and the women's safety assured. Does that answer your question?"

Martin digested the story. It could have been a tale, a fabrication, yet there were many facts that he could verify if he wished to do so.

"Your latest flat is somewhere close to Maggie Thatcher's birthplace?"

"Yes, a two-bedroomed flat I have just obtained. I have it for a year and there are two women in there, who given time and support, can rebuild their lives following their destructive relationships."

"And the brothel?"

"Yes, that was a dark day for the charity. The two women who were living above the launderette decided that working in a sausage packing factory did not bring in enough cash. They continued their employment at the factory, no doubt to ensure my daughter did not suspect anything was amiss. But they craved more and decided that offering sexual services was an easy, if not risky, way to increase their income."

Martin nodded, he now believed Henry and his discreet support of his daughter's charity. He had jumped to a conclusion, an easy and obvious answer which was wrong.

"As you can imagine, there is all sorts of gossip about me and my flats. I think some of those rumours include me having a sort of extra-marital harem, or even a wife-swapping club. I just ignore them all, as you will understand what happens in those flats needs to be kept under wraps. I hope I can trust you in that respect. Plus if you are still doubtful about my story, check the charity commission website, you'll find my daughter's name on a list of trustees."

If he was being honest, Martin felt a fool for thinking even for a short time that Henry Phillips might have been a super pimp. Yet everything he had heard was pointing to that possibility, which he felt was vindication for posing the questions. The two men stood and shook hands.

"My lips are sealed as to the activity of your daughter's charity. I don't think I managed to speak to her at the wedding."

"Maybe you'll get a chance at your own wedding," Henry grinned broadly.

"I don't think I'll be getting hitched in the near future."

"Really? That's not what I imagined. You are with your young lady, Susan."

Immediately Martin corrected the relationship to point out Susan was his co-director. He did not want to create any misunderstandings, there had been enough of those during the weekend.

"Well, between two men, I understand that my daughter and your Susan were having a long chat and women being women, the thought of marriage was brought up by my daughter, suggesting that Susan and you would be the next happy couple. Because, as my daughter pointed out, you are a bit of a catch, which to me sounds very sexist, but us men let those sorts of things go. But your Susan thinks she is not good enough for you, out of her league, I think was the term she used. Better sort things out, Martin my boy, unless you want to break another heart."

As Martin left, he apologised for making such allegations, but hoped the Grantham butcher understood why he had asked about them. They parted both pleased the misunderstanding had been cleared up.

The real winner in this was Martin. He smiled broadly as he returned to his car, mystery solved, box ticked. Not that everything in the garden was rosy. His pressing problem was still Susan, or rather his indecision was a dilemma of his own making.

Chapter 16

It was early in the evening, the bar at the Harby Hall Hotel was now relaxed after the busy weekend with rugby players drinking into the early hours. There was just one lone individual at the bar, sitting on a high stool caressing a cup of coffee. Martin waited patiently for Susan, hoping she was all right. He would not normally worry too much about her, she was world-wise and not much ever seemed to make her miss her step. For him it felt different away from the teeming metropolis, in a small hotel, in a small town on the outskirts of a market town, nestling in the wide-open countryside of south Lincolnshire. Things were changed here, the houses were isolated, there were long distances from the fire station, the police station and the hospital. People in rural areas had to be more independent. He looked at his watch again. Should he call her, it would satisfy his worries, but most likely annoy Susan. He refrained, leaving his phone in his pocket and sipped his coffee instead.

"I thought you would have gone home with your girlfriend by now?"

The question had broken into Martin's thoughts, it was Imogen the barmaid, who was doing an extra shift tonight covering the absence of a fellow worker who had burnt their hand after dropping a hot iron on it. She was pleased that Martin was there as it afforded her the opportunity to thank him again for helping her solve the mystery of her husband and the perfume. She was obviously pleased that he was not having an affair after all, and in her excitement she had confronted him last night about the dance lessons.

He was, she said, a little embarrassed, yet sorry for having caused her to worry about what he might be up to. Then she added that she had another surprise this morning.

"We're going on a cruise, the Caribbean. I have always wanted to go on one but thought we could never afford it. But he told me he has been putting money away for the last three years, saving up for our special anniversary. I'm totally speechless. We're flying out to Florida and then ten days on a ship, he's already booked it. And it's in part thanks to you finding out about his dance classes."

As she walked away, Martin smiled, maybe some relationships are good and last a lifetime. Maybe, he reasoned, you only hear about the bad ones, those that fall apart. They are the ones that you recall, the break-ups, the arguments, the accusations that are slugged out between partners. Those that endure just carry on without any dramas, under the radar, the couples stay together, in love. That was what he sought but had yet to find.

Paula had been a special person in his life, they planned to marry. It was just her plans included wheedling money out of his bank account into hers, until she had enough and walked out on him, leaving him embarrassed and heartbroken. Maybe that was why he had then turned his attention to older married women. They just wanted fun and that suited him fine.

But now as he grew older, he understood that being with someone for the rest of your life could be an advantage. He did not want to spend his twilight years alone, he wanted to share those years and all the years leading up to that point with someone he could both trust and enjoy being with. It was only Susan's warning that there can be many broken relationships along the way until you find your perfect partner, which made him nervous. Yet Henry's comments had neutralised her warning.

How could she think him out of her league, that was just plain stupid. He, of course, knew from talking to her that she viewed him as living in a different class to her and the possibility of any partnership bridging the chasm between classes was uncrossable. A view he did not accept as he thought it was both naive and absurd.

A relationship between two people is not about where they have come from, it is about what destination they want to reach together. That must be the point of it, sharing pain, sharing lives, sharing love. Colin hinted that from the day you say I do, you must do everything in your power to become a couple, moving along the same road in the same direction.

But Martin had already burnt down one of his bridges by telling Susan they were going back to London tonight, something he now regretted saying, now knowing that she did think him a little special. He could just tell her they were staying another night to continue their investigations, but she would suspect an ulterior motive. Understanding Martin and his lack of enthusiasm for working, she would see through his plan and that was something he did not want.

Martin berated himself, he sounded like a lovesick schoolboy, not a mature adult. Maybe that was where he was going wrong, being too mature, being too adult, being too stand-offish. Equally he felt inept when it came to relationships.

What he wanted was an intervention. If Jupiter could burn down houses, then Eros should be able to create a circumstance to help him stay another night.

A voice interrupted his thoughts, a voice he recognised.

"Martin, so glad I managed to find you here still; there's something I want your help with."

A serious-looking Edwin stood alongside him. Maybe, Martin decided, he had been worshiping the wrong set of gods all his life.

Chapter 17

"The woman could not be more insufferable if she tried," Mother called out from the back of the car.

Earlier, Colin had taken great care to pack the suitcases into the boot, as Mother oversaw his efforts. She had then settled in the back of the car with Becky in the front passenger seat. Colin was driving them towards Little Priory Farm and lunch with Mrs Fitzgerald. The lunch appointment had been confirmed as one o'clock. Leaving the hotel at ten-thirty, Mother guessed that they would have time for a milky coffee and slice of cake before arriving for lunch. The satellite navigation system in the car confirmed the timings that she had already worked out.

The task of finding a suitable teashop on the way, fell to Becky. Preferably Mother wanted a small family run tearoom or coffee shop in one of the many market towns they would pass close to on the way to Little Priory Farm. She had made it perfectly clear that she would not be entertaining any of those ghastly chains of coffee shops where you must first queue, then wait ages at the end of the counter for your coffee. Just like a NAAFI canteen, she said, although she had no idea as to what a NAAFI canteen might be like to eat inside, having never served in the armed forces. Mother liked to think that she had sacrificed a lot in her privileged life.

They were almost at Gladstone Teas, which according to the entry on Google maps was both traditional and good value. The picture in Streetview looked to be a perfect match for Mother's requirements. If it did fit that description, Becky and her fellow passengers were not going to find out.

They were perhaps fifteen minutes from Gladstone Teas and their finest selection of English infusions, when the tinny sound of a Nokia ringtone, muffled, yet still audible, emitted from Mother's handbag. She plunged her hand in, shuffled around, pulled out the ancient phone and answered it courteously.

"Not a problem Patricia, we're having a bit of an expedition over the next day or so. I'm around the area anyway. I'm thinking of getting a pied-à-terre to have some respite from the grime of the city, you know how it is, constant traffic. Longing for a little bit of peace and quiet… Same time tomorrow will not be a problem… Looking forward to catching up with you, it has been just too long. Bye."

Mother ensured her phone had disconnected the call, replaced it into her handbag, and made a disparaging comment before adding, "If she thinks she can play the part of the trumped-up lady of the manor to wriggle out of our lunch, she has another think coming. Becky, change of plan, cancel the tearoom."

Which was both useful and a waste of time as Becky had not booked a table in the first place.

"Colleen, take me straight home. I need a change of clothes and a good night's sleep. Hotel rooms have such hard mattresses, I have no idea how anyone actually sleeps in them. I can then arrive for lunch tomorrow better dressed, to show that country bumpkin, Mrs Fitzgerald, just what the true fashions are in town nowadays."

"Are you getting the train tomorrow, Mrs Hayden?"

"Do not be so stupid Colleen, I am employing you for an extra day. Also, can we get a better model of car for the morning? This Ford just will not cut it at Little Priory Farm. My husband always said that Ford was an acronym for Fix Or Repair Daily. Can we get one of those German cars, BM something I think, or better still a Mercedes, they always have a sense of class and decorum about them."

"Would madame like me to hire a Bentley or maybe a Rolls Royce for the day?" Colin ensured he used his best 'manservant' voice for the question, which Mother either did not pick up on, or chose to ignore. Either way the tone was lost on her.

"Do not be so ridiculous Colleen, we all need to do our bit to save the environment, a Mercedes is my concession to that cause."

"M'lady," was all that Colin needed to say for Becky to burst out laughing.

Once Becky had controlled her mirth, she asked if she was right in assuming that Mother wished both of them to take her to lunch the next day at Little Priory Farm. She pointed out that if that was the case, it would be a six-hour round trip, which was a lot of travelling for Mother in a car and would tire her. Becky was concerned and wondered, if after such an exciting weekend, a lunch date with Mrs Fitzgerald might be best postponed until next week. Mother was unyielding.

"I am doing this for my country and Mrs Thatcher; it will be worth the sacrifice."

Becky and Colin looked at each other with resignation.

***

Edwin dragged Martin away from the bar, he wanted secrecy. The two of them occupied a small discreet table in the corner of the dayroom. Predictably refusing the offer of any form of refreshment, Edwin, still wearing his hat with the woodpecker feather in it, began to explain the situation. He urgently needed Martin's help.

It had begun last week, before the wedding, with a telephone conversation with a fellow numismatist, with whom Edwin had traded coins over many years. The friend wanted to know if he had been contacted by a mysterious individual who said they were selling rare coins from a haul that had been discovered recently in Lincolnshire. Edwin had not heard of any such haul of ancient coins being uncovered in his region. It was news to him.

"I, of course, asked him what period the coins were from. Any new find is normally discovered by those people with metal detectors, digging up fields, so I would be interested to know what was found. These findings also help with the local history of the county, indicating where groups of people travelled or settled, but I digress.

"The coins the mystery seller had to offer, were gold nobles from the first reign of Henry VI, extremely rare coins dating from about 1425AD. This was big news for us collectors if such a haul had been uncovered. But I have heard nothing through the normal channels."

Edwin leaned forward, clearly not wanting anyone to overhear their conversation. He continued with the story. His fellow collector had told him that others had also been contacted with the same offer of a gold noble. It appeared that there were several of them, which confounded all the collectors, given that they were believed to be very rare, only a few in existence. The mystery seller explained that a number had been discovered by a mudlark working somewhere on the River Welland, who did not want to share the loot with the landowner. Hence the coins were on offer by private sale at a reasonable price to valued and trustworthy collectors.

Martin frowned; he was not sure what any of this had to do with him. He was about as far away from being a coin collector as one could be. In fact, he tried to live his life with bank cards and Google Wallet, avoiding cash as much as he could. That thought made him consider that in the future, there would be no currency to collect, hence no coin collectors. Maybe they would collect credit card receipts instead, which sounded as much fun as collecting old bus tickets, another hobby that had been erased by technology.

"Are you listening to me?" Edwin snapped Martin away from his abstract thoughts.

"Most certainly Edwin. But what does this have to do with me?"

A lot, as far as Edwin was concerned, who continued with his own lack of involvement, which had upset him.

"I have spent years running a shop and taken a personal interest in coins for many, many years now. Even in my retirement, I am in constant contact with other like-minded people. We are a brotherhood of avid collectors. However, it would seem that I have yet to receive an invitation to purchase one of these highly sought-after coins."

"So you are annoyed that you cannot buy one?" Martin wanted to understand what the old man was trying to say.

"No, not at all, but it's highly significant that I have not been asked. Let me explain."

Edwin did, reaffirming that in the community of currency and coin collectors, he was a highly regarded specialist and a well-known character. Not only for his odd dress sense and eating habits, but because he had spent decades gathering a vast collection of coins and bank notes, as well as a few medals, although the latter were more of a side hobby for him. His own investigation had established that all prominent well-known collectors except himself had had an invitation to purchase the gold nobles. It had all started about six months ago.

A few collectors had succumbed to the temptation and purchased a coin from the reign of Henry VI, and they appeared to be in ownership of a genuine gold coin from that era. If they were real and for sale, Edwin wanted to know why he was never contacted. Whatever list the mystery seller was using it was almost impossible that his name would not appear on it.

"I can think of only one reason I have been kept in the dark over this matter, the seller knows me, and I know the seller. The only explanation that they do not want to meet me is that they must be forgeries. I'm sure that Dave Harvey is behind this scam."

"Whoa! Edwin, that is some leap you have made from not being invited to the party to accusing Dave Harvey. We suspect he might be slipping forgeries into the market, but his alleged fakes are Roman coins, not English ones. Also, you mention gold coins; are these gold nobles actually made from gold?"

"Yes Martin, I would have thought your public-school education would have schooled you to the fact that when something is called gold, namely gold noble, the coin is indeed gold, solid gold."

"That must mean they are worth a fortune?"

"Not for the gold so much, the Henry VI gold noble or annulet issued during his first reign has about seven ounces of gold in it, which today is worth about four or five hundred pounds. However, the coins themselves because they are rare, sell for about seven to eight thousand pounds. If they're real, then they're remarkable, if they're fakes, then there's a lot of profit in each one."

"Eight thousand pounds for an old coin sounds a lot to me. Okay, once again, why are you telling me all this?"

Edwin smiled, "Because you are buying one."

Unfortunately it was not as simple as that for Martin, Edwin's plan was a little more complex than a straightforward purchase.

The plan had already been devised and activated by Edwin. He truly believed that the mysterious seller must know him, and Dave Harvey was his most likely candidate. Through Edwin's contact in Manchester, who had been approached with the offer to purchase a gold noble, a meeting had been arranged for the next day at a location in Grantham, the town where invited interested collectors had to come to examine the coins prior to purchasing. It was simple, Martin would take the place of the Manchester contact and nab the seller who would, without doubt in Edwin's mind, be Dave Harvey. As if that was not bad enough for Martin, the location made matters still worse.

"Let me get this straight," Martin said after hearing the complete plan. "You want me to go into the Grantham McDonald's, go up to the counter, purchase a Big Mac and two large shakes, then find a table, sit down and wait for someone to approach me?"

"I think the flavour of the drinks is down to you, but that is what the man instructed my Manchester friend to do. Sit and wait, then the seller will join you if he feels safe and then you will follow any directions that he or she might give to you. But I am sure Dave Harvey will see you and you will see him, then by Jove we will have him. You must admit Martin, such a clandestine meeting arrangement can only lead you to appreciate that the whole matter is undercover, and to my mind, illegal in some respect. Hopefully the coins are real, that would be exciting."

"But if they are real, then why the shadowy meetings?"

"As I said earlier, the finder should share the proceeds with the landowner and depending on the value, the state gets involved too, dramatically diluting any income for the finder."

"Let's get this clear. You want me to impersonate this collector friend of yours who has already arranged to meet a man in McDonald's to view the gold coin?"

"You do have a lot of questions Martin. It's all really simple, just sit in the seat and wait for the contact to show up."

"But do you want me to buy it because if you do, you are on very thin ice. The man could offer me anything that vaguely resembles a coin, and I would think it was a gold noble."

"Fret not Martin, whatever he offers you, just look at it for a few minutes, act as if you know what you are doing then turn him down. It's all very simple."

"Don't forget Dave Harvey knows me, he could just say he was popping into McDonald's for his lunch or something."

"I very much doubt he will be there in person, too risky for him. It will be one of his minions, I'm sure. Either way we'll have him."

Edwin left a bewildered Martin, now having an alcoholic drink. He was going to stay one more night after all. He was convincing himself that if he had the courage to go into McDonald's alone, then how hard could it be to ask Susan out for a real date?

***

"Have you ever even stepped inside a McDonalds?" Susan asked after Martin had repeated his upcoming mission.

"No, well maybe once after a night on the tiles. I recall for some obscure reason ordering an apple turnover. Burnt my tongue terribly on the damm thing."

"And you said yes to Edwin for this covert mission?"

"Susan, I am meeting a bloke in McDonalds to look at a coin. I have no idea what it should look like, but I am not going to purchase it anyway. We are not going to carry out an exchange of spies. It is simple, it is easy and…"

"And what?"

"You and I get to spend another night in this hotel together," Martin smiled. "I've booked a room for each of us, but at least we can have dinner together."

"Another night here!" There was more than a hint of panic in Susan's voice.

"I thought you would have welcomed the news."

"You told me we were going back to London tonight."

"Yes, but that was before Edwin came up with this hair-brained scheme, as a result we get to stay another night. Free food and toiletries once more," Martin smiled, unable to understand why she was not eager to stay.

"Martin," they were sitting in the now crowded bar, people close by chatting and laughing. Susan moved closer to him and spoke softly in his ear, "I have run out of knickers."

Martin whispered back, "did your parents never advise you to take spare pairs when you go away from home?"

"No," came the curt reply.

"You can always get the hotel to do your laundry. There most likely is a plastic bag in the wardrobe. They often do them overnight."

In hushed tones, hoping to cover the embarrassment and keep the conversation away from other customers, Susan explained, that she had never let anyone else wash her smalls, as she described them. That was the one thing her mother did teach her. Underwear should only be washed by family members; they were not to be seen at a launderette or a laundry.

"Can you turn them inside out?"

"Martin, that is gross! Is that what you have done?"

"No," Martin was mildly hurt that she thought him capable of such an act. "I packed as I always do, six pairs of additional pants and socks, plus two spare shirts, a spare pair of chino trousers, dark blue so they can go with most things."

"You can be such a goody-goody at times," Susan snatched back.

She finished her glass of wine, then looked at her watch before standing up and looking down at him. "I'm off to the shops to purchase some items. I will be back and expect you to treat me to a slap-up dinner with posh wine tonight for the embarrassment you have caused." Her voice was now at a normal level, if any customers had been interested in what she was saying, which they were not, they would have heard her. Then came Martin's reply, "Me pay for dinner just because you forgot..."

"Don't you dare! Martin Hayden, do not say another word." She turned and left the bar, leaving Martin to finish his drink with a big smug smile.

***

During her life, Susan had read a lot of menus. Her favourite was a cocktail menu, followed by one from a fast-food restaurant or at the very least a burger bar. They were simple to understand and full of items which she recognised. The Harby Hall dinner menu was not only for the most part incomprehensible, but it was also very sparse in the selection department.

Though Martin had promised to pay for the meal to compensate her for having to stay another night in Grantham, Susan still felt, given the prices, that they were being ripped off.

"Halibut Battre with an accompaniment of browned salted pomme strips. Isn't that a posh way of saying fish n' chips?"

Martin peered from behind his own menu. "Yes, but it does allow them to charge twice the price of the local chippie."

"Just goes to show you can't always take for granted what you are told."

Placing the menu carefully on the table, Martin looked at Susan with a quizzical look, her statement had confused him.

"Don't you mean you cannot trust the description?"

"No, not the menu, I'm talking about Henry and his girls. Everyone thinking he was running a sex ring in Grantham, and in fact he was helping victims of violence."

She was impressed with the way Henry Phillips was obtaining flats to house women subjected to violence by their partners. Given his status in the town, he was shrugging off the rumours and gossip that was rife after two women he had helped let him down. However she was not pleased that it was the victims who had to move, and made her thoughts very plain to Martin that it was unacceptable to make the victims move house, leave the area, and start a new life. It was almost as if the innocent party was having to bear the consequences of someone else breaking the law.

Her views were strong as she began a tirade on the subject, citing a friend of hers who had suffered physical and mental brutality at the hands of her partner. Gaining strength from friends, she reported the matter to the police, who in turn ensured that the man went to court. He was found guilty, which sounded all very well, but he was not imprisoned and without twenty-four-hour police protection, she was never going to be safe. Her only option was to move away to a destination where no one could find her, not even her friends. Both Susan and Martin agreed the victim was paying the price. A situation that was not right, yet neither could come up with a suitable solution.

"Maybe slice off his hands and cut out his tongue; that could be an answer," Susan offered with a smile.

"I just hope you never get the chance to join the judiciary," Martin replied. "How are your new undies, comfortable?"

"Yes, thank you, both comfortable and clean. Yet I still do not understand why you changed your mind about going back to London tonight, it couldn't have been just to help an old man."

"Why not?"

Martin wondered if this might be a good time to bring up the subject of relationships and how he wanted to spend another night with Susan away from the distractions of their lives in London. He watched her munch her way through a mouthful of the Harby Hall version of fish and chips.

"But you never help anyone unless you have to." Susan waved her fork at Martin, interrupting him as he was about to reply. "No, sorry, that isn't true, if it suits you, you'll help someone out. Like following the barmaid's husband, just to get out of having dinner with your mother."

Ignoring the jibe, Martin continued the conversation in his own way. "I am learning from you that caring for my fellow citizens can be rewarding."

"That's what I said, rewarding for you. So why the extra night? These rooms are not cheap, a bit like these fish and chips."

Apart from this not being the right time for the real reason, Martin was struggling to find the right words. Asking someone out who you have just picked up at a bar or the theatre is one thing. Getting intimate and close to a work colleague is something that takes a little more care.

Currently with Susan, they worked in each other's pockets, knew lots about each other and were almost as close as a brother and sister. In his mind Martin began with, 'Susan, I think we should start going out, become lovers.' That was going to be too blunt and a little weird, make him sound like a dirty old man. 'Susan, I think our relationship should move to the next level.' All very well but Martin had no idea exactly what level they might consider themselves to be on at the present time and so what would the next one be. 'Susan, shall we go out?' Not obvious enough as technically tonight they were going out. Martin put off the discussion in his mind, citing the fact that such a topic should really be left until the meal has been finished. Delay for now.

"Well, I suppose having just spoken to Henry Phillips, knowing what good work he was doing, it was obvious now that Edwin knew the truth, so he must be a trusted friend of Henry's. I guess I thought it was the right thing to do, help the old man out. It should not be an onerous task, and I think it will put me in the good books with the Phillip's family."

"Why be in their good books? You hardly know the family, only Howard."

"Yes, but Edwin's pride has been hurt, at least I can help him restore some of it. Look Susan, shall we get another bottle of wine?"

It was a well-used tactic of Martin's if any conversation with Susan was not going in the direction that he wanted it to, he would either offer her a drink, or ask about his horoscope. It worked. Well, to a point, until Susan said that she would join him at McDonald's.

"But you need someone as a back-up," Susan protested as the waiter brought another bottle of wine to their table.

"Susan, I am going to meet a crooked coin dealer in McDonald's. The only danger I face will be the amount of cholesterol in the Big Mac. There is no need for you to be there. In fact, if this dealer is who Edwin thinks it is, then there is a good chance Dave Harvey will recognise me and just walk off or at least be polite."

"But all good detectives have back-up when doing these clandestine meetings. I can be discreet."

"One, we are not good detectives, two, as I mentioned, I do not need back up, and three, you cannot be discreet if you tried."

"Well, I think you are making a mistake. Do you really think that Dave is selling the coins?"

Martin, if he was honest with himself, did not really know. He cared even less. He rolled his own Roman coin between his fingers; he had kept it as a talisman since he had found it. He tried to explain to Susan that it is not so much if the coin is real or not, the question is, are you, the customer, satisfied with your purchase.

Buying a coin off the internet which has been described as one from the Roman Empire, you might be paying ten pounds for it. When you get it, unless you are an expert with access to facilities, there would be little hope of you actually finding out if it was original. Carbon dating costs a fortune, he pointed out to Susan.

Hence it was not so much if it was genuine, more if you were happy to accept it as an item and felt you had good value for money. Real or not, it does not matter. Even when Susan highlighted the bad reviews that the church pushed down the web page, Martin was happy to point out that if you looked at any best seller on Amazon, there would always be some bad reviews. You can't please all the people all the time. Dave was no doubt satisfying the majority of his customers and that in the end was all that counted.

However, Martin did accept that if Dave Harvey was selling fake coins for several thousand pounds, then he hoped that the standard of the fakes was good enough to convince the dealer that the item they were getting was the real thing. There again, if they wanted to take the time and trouble to carbon date the coins, then that was up to them.

"How did Rodney and Tracey meet in the first place?" Martin asked once he had finished his dessert, a rather lacklustre strawberry tart, with a boule of ice cream.

Susan had also finished her dessert, 'Pomme Pastry Paradise', which was apple pie with a spoonful of custard, what it lacked in size Susan thought it made up for in quality.

She had found out that Rodney and Tracey had first met each other at an evening class. What she did not know or think to ask, was the first question that Martin asked her.

"What subject were they studying?"

"Missed that bit, we got diverted onto why she ended up going out with him. Tracey seemed to think, him being a mummy's boy, he was ripe to be mothered by her. It was some weird instinct she seemed to think she had. Doomed to failure, she decided in the end."

"Do you think I'm a mummy's boy?"

"Christ no Martin, far from it. I'm not saying that when she dies you're not going to be upset and shed a few tears, but your world will not crumble around you. Plus, you can afford to get someone to do your laundry and clean the house, something Rodney could not."

"I'm glad you feel that way. I'd hate to think that someone was going out with me just because they were being kind and sympathetic."

This was the opening Martin was waiting for. The conversation moving into the area of relationships and reasons to go out together. He did not really like Rodney, but he would have liked to say thank you for helping him in this instance.

'In that case, say you were to go out with me in a romantic sense, what would be the magnetism drawing you to me, if not sympathy and kindness?' It was not going to win any prizes for chat-up lines, of that Martin was sure, but it would move the conversation in the right direction. Well, it would have done, except all he managed to say was, "In that case..." before Susan's phone, which was sitting on the table beside her rang.

Listening to Susan's phone discussions was entertaining. Martin tried, as a sort of game, to work out what the other party was saying, in most cases he was wrong.

"No way, after they agreed it. Just goes to show how vindictive people can be... Well I suppose she doesn't want to give up. She's a tenacious old girl and that's a fact... Again tomorrow... I wouldn't have bothered, I'd just write a couple of letters and seen what happens, but I never liked the woman anyway... No, we're back tomorrow, you know Martin once he gets his teeth into an investigation, there's no stopping him," Susan laughed which Martin thought rather unkind.

Susan finished the conversation, looked at Martin and smiled. He spoke first,

"One of your girlfriends having man trouble?" which was more than often the case.

"Wrong, your mother was turned down for lunch today so she's back in the area tomorrow to sort out her posh friend and get a statue for dear old Maggie. I thought you'd be pleased."

"Fortunately," Martin pointed out, "the Fitzgerald place is a good few miles south of here. There is very little chance of Mother and I crossing paths until we are both back in London."

"See, no way are you a mother's boy."

Chapter 18

There was no denying that as the automatic door slid open, Martin was beyond his comfort zone. He stood frozen to the spot for a moment assessing his surroundings. He concluded it was a maelstrom of colour, noise, people and an odd aroma which he could not quite place, or decide where it might have originated from. He considered the self-service screens, which seemed to be attracting a lot of interest from customers. As tempted as he was, he dismissed that option, deciding it would be a lot safer to speak to a real person to ensure he received exactly what he had been asked to order. Unless he had the correct contents laid out on his tray, this mystery seller would probably not approach or speak to him.

He moved through the bustle of people and found himself at a counter, behind which was a short woman in a brown McDonald's uniform, she looked up at him and warmly smiled.

The server looked overly pleased that someone had decided to take advantage of her encyclopaedic knowledge of the McDonald's menu, forsaking the inanimate touch screen ordering system. She had hated those structures ever since the company introduced them. Not only did it mean that there were less colleagues and customers at the counter, but she also had to clean the screens at regular intervals, which seemed a little demeaning to her, especially as she had to stand on a small step to reach the top.

"What can I get you?" she asked courteously of the man who looked like a rabbit caught in the headlights.

"A Big Mac and two large shakes please."

"What flavour do you want?"

It was an obvious question to a regular at the Golden Arches, but Martin was not a member of that huge group. "Well, I suppose a normal Big Mac will be fine. They are real beef, aren't they?" He had always suspected that McDonald's was in fact a glossy version of an old-fashioned burger bar, asking about what flavour burger he wanted was throwing that assumption into doubt.

Luckily for Martin, the short crew member took pride in her knowledge of the products, often boring her fellow workers with her unhealthy interest as to what exactly went into them.

"Our Big Mac is in fact one hundred percent beef, two meat patties, a slice of cheese as well as crisp lettuce, not forgetting onion and pickles plus that super sauce. We can, of course, remove any of those items should you not desire the standard Big Mac."

There had to be something in that detailed list of ingredients that needed a flavour choice, it was just Martin could not think which part it might be. Sensing a person now standing behind him, he wanted to bring this conversation to a conclusion and get on with the main purpose of his visit, the clandestine meeting.

"What would you recommend?" A question Martin had often used when dining out with family and friends. Waiters always offered wise suggestions, not so McDonald's crew members.

"Chocolate every time for me." The short McDonald's girl wondered if this nice man was flirting with her, she hoped so.

"Chocolate?"

"Well, I am partial to chocolate milkshakes, maybe you fancy that one, otherwise in addition we have strawberry, banana or vanilla."

"Ah, milkshakes." Martin heard a tutting sound behind him. "Chocolate will be fine for both drinks."

With an immense feeling of relief Martin finally sat down at a table. It did not have a real chair, instead he had to sit on a round plastic brightly covered pouffe on a pole, which did not move in the slightest as it was screwed to the floor. Martin wondered if that was to deter the people of Grantham stealing them. Once he had settled himself, he realised that on the plastic tray the short crew member had given to him, there was no sign of any napkins. He looked around, saw the condiment station and collected a handful. After returning to his red pouffe and removing the lid of the milkshake, he soon recognised that a straw was needed. Once more he returned to the condiment station, collected two straws, a small tub of tomato sauce, a small tub of brown sauce, which turned out not to be brown sauce, as well as a handful of salt and pepper sachets. He had no intention to leave his table again until the mysterious seller sat down.

Trying to make himself look at home in the environment, he sucked on a straw to taste the recommended chocolate milkshake, nothing happened. He sucked harder, nothing happened. Just to be sure he pulled the straw out of the brown paste to confirm that it was not blocked. Martin likened the experience of sucking on a McDonald's milkshake as the reverse of trying to blow up a balloon, both life threatening unless you have a compressor handy or lungs the size of airships. He left the cold drink in the hope that it would in time melt into a liquid consistency. The Big Mac proved to be a tad easier, but not a lot. The size of the double decker burger was more than Martin's mouth could cope with to bite cleanly. The top burger slid outwards away from his mouth, the sauce dripped down on the table and the tomato simply just fell out. He put the Big Mac down and wiped his mouth, wishing Edwin had arranged that he should just sit in the restaurant with a simple coffee.

Martin looked around, not keen to continue eating or drinking, neither of which he was finding to be easy. There was a spectrum of humanity in the place. Children were present, but not in the majority, some pensioners sitting chatting, workmen in their grubby overalls and jackets. Some business-suited young men, rushing out with their meal in a bag. Plus, a couple of what Martin suspected were delivery personnel, with insulated bags, ready to ride off on their mopeds to a residential home and deliver a meal of burgers and shakes. He had heard of such things, as yet he had not tried such a service, which he felt in time, with Susan beside him, he would have to endure. However there was no sign of anyone who might be there for a clandestine meeting, only himself, who must be looking suspicious by now, having sat for the best part of fifteen minutes and still only half eaten his Big Mac and without enough breath to drink either of his two chocolate milkshakes.

"You're the private detective, aren't you?"

Martin had to be honest with himself, that was not a phrase anyone who was working undercover awaiting a highly sensitive meeting with a dealer of alleged illegal goods, wanted to hear. He looked at the man, holding a milkshake and a brown bag, who without waiting for an invitation from him, sat on the green screwed down pouffe opposite. Martin recognised the man as Imogen's dancing husband.

"And you're Reggie, as I recall?"

"Spot on. Fancy seeing you here, just popped in for my lunch and thought, that's the bloke who turned up at the dance class. I'm glad I bumped into you. I wanted to say thank you."

"For what?" Martin felt he was all at sea in a force ten gale. Apart from being in a fast-food restaurant to partake in a clandestine rendezvous, he was now talking to a man whom he had thought he had observed surreptitiously. Clearly not.

"Helping my wife work out what I was up to. She told me everything. She was so excited about me being able to dance with her at our forthcoming anniversary, she couldn't help but tell me she had sent an investigator to see what I was up to." Reggie laughed loudly, his whole body shaking. "I never smelt the perfume on me, I suppose I was oblivious to it. Lucky I wasn't really having it off with some other woman. So yeah, thanks. I gather you helped her out free of charge, which was really kind of you."

Reggie stopped talking and took a large mouthful from his drink, with an ease that made Martin vaguely jealous.

"No need for thanks, I was just helping your wife allay her fears," Martin admitted. He did not own up that he did it to avoid dinner with his mother, that might have been difficult to explain to a stranger.

"I have even confessed to her that I'm taking her on a cruise, which she has always dreamed of. To be honest I'm not that keen, bit like being on a prison hulk I imagine, but she wants it, so what more can a man ask? You must understand, with you being married as well."

"I'm not married," Martin corrected quickly.

"Oops, sorry. I assumed that the woman you were with was your wife, she seemed very comfy in your arms, very relaxed."

"No, she is my employee, well sort of."

"Ah, now I get your drift, a bit on the side."

"No!" The accusation hurt Martin, as if he would ever use Susan as a bit on the side. "She is a close friend and a very able investigator, like me."

"Sorry, maybe I should keep my thoughts to myself, even so thank you both in that case."

"Well, it was good of you to tell me that you and your wife have sorted it out, but as you can see, I am waiting for someone." Martin indicated the two drinks wanting to conclude this pointless conversation.

"Sorry, I'll be on my way and thanks again." Then Reggie was off, out through the automatic door as he impressively sucked strongly on his milkshake, leaving Martin alone and waiting.

***

Neither Reggie nor Martin had seen the man, in fact, nobody had noticed him, that was his speciality. You could pass him in the street and never see him, he just appeared to be a part of the white noise of town life. Today he was just another anonymous diner, a mere shadow, yet he was far from that, he was at work. As he entered the fast-food restaurant, his eyes darted around looking for his target. He saw Martin sitting, looking very lost in his surroundings. Automatically he walked past the self-serve touch screens, ignored the counter and headed for a person he had already singled out, a young woman ending her lunch hour, walking with a tray full of debris from her meal. Politely he smiled, snatching the tray from her.

"I'll take it." He did not wait for an answer. He took the tray, with its empty wrappers, half-drunk coffee and deserted cold chips, found himself an empty table and sat down. He now looked to anyone passing by as a man who had just finished his meal, not someone who had just arrived and had little interest in eating.

His purpose for being in this diner had nothing to do with satisfying his hunger, it was all about Martin. That was his person of special interest. He saw Martin with his two drinks, talking with someone else. It was a man he partly recognised but he could not be sure of his identity. The two of them were chatting. Martin looked tense, whereas the other man seemed relaxed, an odd contrast. It was not what he had anticipated while he waited outside the hotel for Martin to leave. If he had to be honest, he was now not sure what today might bring.

If only he could recall who Martin was talking to. He was convinced he knew him from somewhere, but where? If he could answer that question, then he might be able to discover the reason Martin was holding a meeting in McDonald's.

He watched as the man stood up and left Martin alone. To be safe, the man dropped a napkin and bent down to pick it up, he did not want to be recognised. Taking his time, he watched the feet walk past him and move away.

He remained sitting, with his borrowed debris on a tray, for another ten minutes, before he observed Martin standing with his tray, burger uneaten and no doubt drinks left untouched. Two drinks, so presumably his previous guest could not have been the person he was intending to meet. That man, who he still could not recall, walked out holding his own drink and brown bag of food. As Martin went to one recycling point, the man went to another, ensuring that his back was to Martin all the time. He held back, waiting for Martin to leave, then he continued watching him through the glass, until he met up with a woman, his accomplice. He recognised her without any trouble.

***

"What on earth are you doing here?" Martin asked.

Susan opened her arms wide as if she was going to greet him with a big hug, of which she had no intention of doing. It was more of an admission of remorse, even so, she raised a wide grin.

"Watching out for my partner."

"Susan, we are not Starsky and Hutch and this is most certainly not Bay City California, this is Grantham."

"You mean I can't be your Huggy Bear?"

"Whatever that means Susan, I would say no."

"That might be so, but nonetheless I had your back, because I saw you make contact with the dealer. Who'd have thought it was the dancing husband?"

"His name is Reggie, and he is not the mysterious seller of gold coins. He is a grateful husband, thanking us for saving his marriage, or his face, not sure which. My visit to McDonald's was a waste of time on many levels. It did not go as planned."

"Ah," the disappointment in Susan's voice was palpable. "Well, we tried."

"No Susan, we did not try; I tried; you gate-crashed this happening. Where exactly were you? Standing here in the middle of the car park for all to see?"

"No, actually I was over there," she pointed behind her, "outside the Spar supermarket watching out for you."

"By the Spar supermarket, which is at least fifty yards away with a low fence in between. What use would you have been if I had been attacked and left for dead on the floor of McDonald's?"

Susan pondered the question for a moment, playing the scenario in her mind. "I would have given you the last rites."

"Are you qualified for such a thing?"

"No, but you'd be dead anyway and wouldn't know a thing about it. Let's move on from fictitious situations. What now?"

"I guess we tell Edwin it has not gone to plan, no one contacted me."

At that point, intruding on their discussion, Martin's phone began to ring, it was an agitated Edwin. Once Martin had finished the call and had returned the phone to his pocket, he took out his car keys and walked towards his car. Susan as he expected followed him.

"That was Edwin. Apparently, our coin seller has contacted the potential Manchester buyer, who in turn has passed the message onto Edwin and he has forwarded what was said to me. A sort of Chinese whispers. It would seem the man selling the gold coins believes he was being set up. Putting, and I quote, 'a gumshoe' in place of the buyer. The deal has been called off."

"He saw you and knew you were a detective?"

"It would seem so, and in my books if the person knew me, then I must have met them in the last couple of days, as I do not normally frequent the streets of Grantham, why would I? There is only one person I know who has called me a gumshoe."

"Vera!" Susan exclaimed, as she got into the car with Martin. They drove out of the car park.

***

From the automatic doorway of McDonald's, the man, apart from causing congestion in the entrance, watched Martin with his sidekick drive out of the car park, turn left, then stop at the traffic lights. He wondered where they were going now. If they were heading for the town centre, then following might become difficult. Nevertheless, he had to try, it was pointless giving up now. He ran back to his car, started the engine and aggressively forced his way into the waiting traffic and was just two cars behind Martin as the lights turned green.

***

Number three Hayling Buildings, Warburton Street, Grantham, was in Martin's honest judgement a dilapidated post war building that had suffered from years of neglect and under-resourced management, leaving the two-storey building less than desirable. Susan just called it a shit hole.

However you might decide to describe the small ragged estate, this was where Vera lived. Martin banged hard on the door, hoping to get an answer. Before leaving McDonald's, he had called Howard to get the address of his 'Auntie Vera' which came with the warning, 'only pay cash for your weed'.

Impressing Susan, Martin had recalled that Vera had used the term gumshoe at the wedding. Believing it to be an odd, almost extinct description of a private detective, Susan guessed that she could well be the coin seller. She would have walked into the Golden Arches fast food restaurant expecting to see a stranger from Manchester sitting alone with two milkshakes, only to see Martin sitting there, waiting. She would have recognised him at once, turned tail and ran. In her call she let slip the vital clue, gumshoe.

In fact, even Martin was smug with his own deduction. It made him feel good. Once again, he banged heavily on the door of number three.

Vera appeared at the door holding a chipped mug full of milky tea and a scowl on her face. She was wearing a loose-fitting pair of leggings that had several small holes in them, the white of her flesh contrasting against the washed-out black material of her leggings. Her top was a heavily stained pink hoodie with the zip halfway down or halfway up, depending on your viewpoint of life. The perspective the gapping hoodie gave was of a frayed bra that had seen better days.

"Come for that spliff?" She smiled as she scratched her crotch.

"No," Martin made clear. "We wanted to have a chat with you about old coins."

"Well, you'd better come in then, not that I have any idea what 'old coins' is about but I guess it will be fun." She turned, leaving the door open for them to follow her into the flat, farting as she walked.

Her place was nothing more than a small bedsit. They walked into the one big room, that had a sink and small cooker under the Crittall window, with black mould along the metal frames. The unmade bed dominated the sparse room, which had a small table and one chair in the corner beside a grimy door, which Martin hoped would lead to a bathroom. From the odour of human sweat, he guessed that any bath or shower beyond the door would not have seen a lot of use.

"I'd offer you a seat, but I have only the one. You can have the chair," Vera said looking at Susan, "I'll sprawl on the bed with your boyfriend," she leered.

Both Susan and Martin made it clear that they were more than happy to stand, and Martin, not wanting to remain a second longer than he had to in this place, began at the deep end with the blunt question of, 'Are you selling Henry VI coins?'

To which Vera responded that she had no idea who Henry the sixth was, but if he was living in Grantham then she might well have known him at some time. Susan then tried pointing out that gold coins from the reign of that king were being sold and they wanted to know if she was selling them on the black market. Before Vera had a chance to answer, Susan continued, she had just remembered something.

"When did King Henry the sixth reign?"

"What's all this, are we doing a mastermind quiz?" Vera replied, "I have trouble remembering the name of the king before Queen Liz, how should I know?"

Martin contributed what he could recall about Henry VI, which was not a great deal.

"I know he reigned twice and he had one son. Oh, he was also the only monarch to have been crowned King of France. Why the interest?"

Once again, Vera concluded that her two visitors were speaking a type of patois that she really did not understand, but if they wanted a threesome, smoke some dope or just get totally pissed, she would happily get involved with that.

Susan googled King Henry on her phone and soon discovered that he was on the throne from 1422-1461 then from 1470-1471. Martin, haughty about being right, was ignored by Susan as she explained.

"The book in Rodney's bedside cupboard: Medieval coins, any coins from King Henry's reign would have been in there, he was doing research."

"Oh, that posh book. Odd thing I thought for Rodney with him being a little short in the intelligence stakes. But I'm still missing your point."

"How did you know about the book? It was at the back of his bedside cupboard," Susan queried Vera.

"I saw it when I was poking around in there after he had gone to work."

"You rummaged around his personal possessions? That's a bit off." Susan was genuinely surprised that Vera would search through Rodney's belongings while he was out.

"Look dearie, we had cardinal knowledge of each other, I think that gives me the right to see what he has stashed away."

"I think you mean carnal knowledge," Martin helpfully pointed out.

"Whatever, we were shagging, so we should have no secrets."

"But you were a secret to his girlfriend," Susan reminded Vera.

"That was what he chose. You know me, free love and open relationships, but he wanted it kept quiet. So it got a bit heated when she turned up once whilst we were at it. She was a mad bitch, maybe he was scared of her. She had no sense of sharing, it's not as if he was married to her. But, oh so posh. She got real nasty."

Having first offered it to her guests, both of whom refused, Vera lit a spliff. She then went on at great length describing what Rodney liked to do in bed, and which his girlfriend was not willing to partake. The description at one point became so graphic, Martin felt a little bit sick as he tried not to picture the scene she was painting for them. The upshot was, even when Vera was happy to share Rodney and her own slightly unhygienic body with the girlfriend, she was refused. Martin could understand that Tracey, even with her grimy hands, no doubt had certain standards, however low they might be considering she was dating Rodney.

Discretion wasn't in Vera's vocabulary as she continued to talk about Rodney's girlfriend. "Take the time she burnt the house down."

Martin's and Susan's ears pricked up.

"She, you mean Tracey set light to the house?" Martin asked to be sure Vera was not using the term as a euphemism.

"Yeah. Me and Roddy had just had an afternoon session before he was off to work on one of his late turns. He'd called me in the morning, 'Vera, I'm horny, can you come over?'"

Martin was happily reassured that the golden age of romance had not yet died in this leafy corner of England.

"Well, I popped along, glad to help out. Then we does our doings and he has to go to work, leaving me in the house alone, telling me to let myself out when I was ready. I slept for a bit then woke dying for a pee and went for one in the bathroom. There I was sitting on the bog, knickers around me ankles, when I hear footsteps. Then someone calls out, 'Rodney you around?' Well at once I recognise the voice, it's the mad bitch girlfriend. I grab a pair of scissors just in case and waits. Then there's the smashing of glass, things being broken, a right commotion, somewhere close to the bog. Then silence, and then I hear her going back downstairs. I still hold up in the bog, no way was I wanting to confront her. Then a few moments later the front door slams. I was relieved, I can tell you, I'm not one for fighting. I'd stick up for meself, but I'd hate a fight. Still, she had gone. I pull up me knickers and leggings, peek out of the bathroom, all is clear. Well, the state of the bedroom, you should have seen it. Broken glass and ripped-up photos, all his clothes strewn over the floor. Then what happens, I smell burning. I go downstairs and the fucking front room is ablaze, time for me to depart pronto, no point hanging around. Mind, I'm a responsible person, so before I go, I calls nine nine nine from the kitchen phone. I tell them the place is ablaze, give them the address, then run off out the back and lose myself."

"Why didn't you tell the police about this?" Susan asked.

"Yeah right, me go off to speak to the bobbies and what do they do? Take me statement, pleased I could help them. Oh by the way, about this stuff you have," she brandished the half-smoked spliff. "They'd lock me up for this and then do a section eighteen and search this place, which at the time had a little more than personal use weed on the premises. No way was I going to get turned over just because I was doing a good deed and grassing up that mad bitch."

"Did you tell Rodney about Tracey burning down his house?"

"I did, but not then. The day after the fire, I hooked up with this guy, he was up here fishing, spent three days beside the river, fishing and shagging. It was fun until he decided he needed to go back up north to his wife. So it was about a week later I mentioned it to Roddy, by that time the insurance company were already onto the case. He didn't seem surprised. But then I hear he's blaming Jupiter and I don't mean that yappy little dog of his."

Martin looked at Vera. A mother and ex-wife, a woman in her sixties he guessed, doing the sort of things that kids do, sleep around, take drugs, drink excessively, have no sense of responsibility. He wondered how someone who arrived at her time of life is able to do such things. Maybe it was because it was after the weekend, possibly it was just Martin was losing touch with the real world, that he asked her, "Vera, why are you at your age acting like a rebellious teenager?"

Being called a rebellious teenager was something new for Vera. Her antics, politics, personal habits and promiscuous relationships had most often been described by those of a similar age to her, as her being a stupid old woman who should never have divorced her husband. Others put it down to her hormonal imbalance. The consensus was she had lost the plot of living a normal life. She liked the idea of being a rebellious teenager.

The way Martin had described her was exactly what she felt, an unruly teenager, something that she never had the opportunity to be. Both her parents were very strict, very domineering and used her as a captive held under their collective thumbs.

This suffocating discipline led her to marrying her first husband when she was only eighteen. The first chance she had to be herself, make her own decisions. The choice she made was not the best, well, she had not been given the chance to practice much. Her first husband, who she thought she loved, had just one flaw, he thought the word fidelity had something to do with the sound system that he used to shatter the neighbour's peace. Hence faithfulness was not one of his traits. Vera was patient with him, why not, she did not want to admit to her gloating parents that she had made a mistake. After the seventh affair, she gave up and went back to her parents and endured their 'told you so's'.

Her next husband was always faithful to her. He was not righteous; he was just too lazy to find himself another woman, which after the first couple of years of marriage, Vera wished he would. In the end Vera endured thirty years with the sloth.

Bearing him two children, his involvement did not go beyond the conception. Vera, cleaned, cooked, washed, shopped, soothed, scolded and saved a few pennies for the kids toys. Then she had to take a part-time job to help ends meet, while her husband lazed on a chair waiting for his meals to arrive. Thirty years of marriage and Vera had not once done anything for herself.

Once their two children had left home, Vera joined the exodus, leaving hubby clutching the divorce papers. She was now ready to live her life to the full, doing exactly what she wanted, whenever she wanted, with whoever she wanted.

"I'm now in my sixties," she reminded her guests, inhaled deeply on her joint, then exhaled slowly. "That means I have more years behind me than in front, and that's why I'm getting on with living. I'm not asking for anyone's approval, so their disapproval I accept and ignore, as I get on with living life my way." Vera smiled, she could see both Martin and Susan saw her point of view.

***

Once Susan was sitting alongside Martin in his car, there was one question she asked before he had closed the car door. "What exactly did she mean by, 'does our doings'?"

"I cannot recall that phrase being in any dictionary that I have consulted, but I presumed, rightly or wrongly, that she was referring to her and Rodney having sex. It seemed to fit where the general conversation was going."

"Well, I've never heard of it before."

"Have you ever had sex in Grantham before?"

Susan paused and thought for longer than Martin might have expected before she answered, "No."

"In that case it could well be the phrase they use around here for doing it."

"I'll ask Colin when I see him. He's about the same age as her, it could be an old people thing. Where to next?"

That was a good question Martin thought. The wedding had long concluded, so what was he still doing in Grantham? Being kind to his elders, Martin decided.

Even if at the very start, Martin had felt a little sorry for Rodney, that compassion had now been eroded away. The man was no doubt spending most of his waking hours planning to be something he was never going to be. Seeing the world through his eyes for his own purpose. If he was lying about his girlfriend, he was no doubt telling a few other fibs every time he opened his mouth. As for his ex-girlfriend, well serves her right for taking up with the man in the first place. Plus, anything she said could no doubt be taken with a pinch of salt. Broken relationships do that.

As for the rumours and allegations surrounding Dave Harvey, Martin put those in the same group as the accusations about Henry Phillips and his string of sex workers. All false. Even if Dave was peddling fake Roman coins, Martin did not really care, there was a reason Trading Standards existed.

Edwin was the only reason that Martin had remained in town. Not because he was bothered if fake King Henry coins were being sold, more out of respect for Edwin. He was prepared to put himself out and dig around a little for Edwin's concerns. Martin believed that you should always respect your elders, unless they happened to be an interfering mother.

"We can assume that the man came into McDonald's hoping to sell his gold coin, saw me, knew I was a detective, or gumshoe to use his term, therefore he has seen or met me at some point this weekend. That puts a lot of names in the frame. But he must also have access to a supply of gold. Where does one buy gold in Grantham?" Martin paused, Susan remained silent, then he continued, "Like you, I have no idea, but I know a man who should, Reggie Miller, our dancing husband, didn't his wife mention he is a jeweller?"

"I think you're really getting the hang of this detecting lark, plus it can't be far as he popped in for his lunch. I'll Google jewellers around here."

A few moments later they had their answer.

"Miller Jewellery, other side of town. Mind," Susan pointed out, "with only one McDonald's in this place, I'd drive over here for lunch."

Martin pulled away from Warburton Street, unaware that the car behind him was the same one that had followed him out of McDonald's. In the same way, the driver of the car behind, could not understand why Martin and Susan had visited a downbeat flat on the Hayling Buildings, to his mind one of the worst places in Grantham.

They must have a reason, which might become clear once they got to their next destination.

Chapter 19

Not since he was a police detective had Colin needed to set his alarm for such an unearthly morning hour. Even so, he did not resent it; he had a lot to do. First, wear something suitable for the day ahead. He chose a smart trouser suit, wanting to project a formal look yet nothing too official. He might have been allocated the job of chauffeur by Mrs Hayden, but he was not going to look like one. The trousers were a turquoise green, high-waisted with a wide leg style. The matching blazer was single-breasted with a notch collar. Under this he wore a long-sleeved striped woman's shirt.

He collected the keys to the Mercedes C Class, ignored the looks he got from the rental staff, slipped the car into drive and made his way to collect Becky, who had unsurprisingly overslept. She had thrown on a pair of distressed jeans, a leopard print top and a leather jacket. None of the items met with Colin's approval, so he sent her back indoors to rectify her fashion crime. If they were going to meet one of Mother's counterparts, then he was going to ensure that the 'hired helpers' looked respectable and suitable.

Becky thought he was being testy. She changed into a very smart, neatly pressed navy-blue business jacket with matching skirt. Even the modest fake pearls, added to the impression that she was a serious business executive preparing to launch a take-over of a rival company, not go to lunch with a couple of old biddies and a transvestite.

The journey was conducted mostly in silence, Becky and Colin avoiding the casual gossip they liked to indulge in.

Mother was still jaded after the weekend. As much as she would like to have put this luncheon off, she was not going to lose face in front of Mrs Fitzgerald, plus she was on a mission to get a statue for Mrs Thatcher. All three of them had the sense that they were about to partake in some form of combat.

Little Priory Farm was well sign-posted, assisting the numerous tourists that made their way to the neatly trimmed gardens that the once-working farm was now renowned for. It was a favoured haunt for gentle ladies to spend time together and chat while their husbands were playing golf. The average visitor would walk beside their companion through the gardens praising the floral displays, marvelling at the care the gardeners lavished on the shrubs. Then they would settle down at a table in the celebrated tea rooms, that were once stables for the working horses. There they would sit drinking tea, nibbling neatly cut, yet expensive sandwiches and sharing spiteful chitchat with each other.

Colin parked the Mercedes, as per Mrs Hayden's instructions, at the quiet end of the gravel laid car park, far from the main entrance and ticket office for the gardens. They were parked close to a gate set in a carefully trimmed privet hedge, simply marked 'Private'. Beyond the gate were neat flower beds, with squares of grass, manicured to create the impression the grass was artificial. The cottage, the garden of which they were walking through, was thatched and traditionally quaint, it was the sort of cottage you would find portrayed on a jigsaw or biscuit tin.

Mother tugged on the metal rod that in turn rattled a small high-pitched bell. A few moments later a woman opened the door and warmly greeted her old friend with a hug and an air kiss on each cheek.

"My darling, it has been simply too long. The fault is mine, but the gardens take up so much of my time. I have lunch all prepared. Lovely rollmops, your favourite, see I remember." It was then that Patricia Fitzgerald turned her attention to the two people standing patiently behind Mrs Hayden. "Who are these people?"

"This is Becky, my personal assistant and Colleen, my driver, both are wonderful and so compassionate to my wants."

"Colleen?" Patricia looked at the driver dressed in a very casual trouser suit, whose features looked very masculine. She wanted to ask, but refrained, deeming the sexuality of a driver overall irrelevant and that it was of little interest to her who Mrs Hayden wanted to employ. "And Becky, pleased to meet you both." In fact, she was horrified these two helpers were standing at her doorstep, no doubt expecting to be invited to join them for lunch. That was not what she had planned and that certainly was not going to happen.

"I can sort out some refreshments in the garden tea rooms for your help," Patricia spoke to Mother, not wanting to address the helpers directly. "If they follow this path," she indicated a row of round stepping stones that led towards the public gardens. "I'll ensure they are catered for."

"Becky, I'll call when I am ready to go," Mother called out, as Becky and Colin followed the directions along the stepping stones, both muttering under their breath, "Yes m'lady"

It was no doubt a well-worn path from the picturesque cottage where Mrs Fitzpatrick lived to the garden tea rooms, aptly named Patricia's Pantry. Years of hired help had moved through the gardens to take their refreshments apart from their employers. Once Becky and Colin arrived, they were quickly supplied with sandwiches, pots of tea, glasses of water and a comfortable table away from the counter.

"I bet your careers advisor never pointed out the advantages of being a hired help," Colin suggested, enjoying a small tasty cheese and ham sandwich.

"If you think about it, that must be one of the worst jobs going. Sitting in a classroom, telling kids what great careers are out there, fortunes to be made, fame and glory thrown in as well. And they, as careers advisors, are stuck in a job which I don't think has any sort of promotion, I never recall anyone being told a careers advisor was a good life choice."

"Maybe that's because it's the best job going," Colin responded with a smile, as he watched Becky's face curl into a frown of non-comprehension. "Put it this way Becky, he looks at your exam results, suggest you become, say a research chemist. You believe everything he tells you and go off and pursue that career, which after ten long years you think is totally stupid and having been in the first team at football, you wish you'd stuck to your dream of being a professional football player. Sadly, that train has long left the station once you're in your thirties. Now you try getting a refund on his advice or recompense. That will not happen. Being a careers advisor is a job which you can never get wrong. Easy money for spouting rubbish."

Becky nodded, acknowledging that point of view was a fair description, as her own career advice was equally useless. She had always wanted to be a nurse; she liked the idea of helping people and that was something her grandpappy always encouraged. Even though at school she was good at maths, her careers advisor assured her that shop work would be a very useful career to follow. It would enable the young Becky to earn money before she was married, marrying being something Becky had no plans to do. The advice continued, once married, she could then easily leave the retail industry and have her family, again which she had no plans to do, before she was advised in the fullness of time return to retail, first part time, then once the children that Becky did not plan to have, were of a certain age, to go back to retail to work full time.

It turned out that the overweight careers advisor, who always wore the same permanently stained suit, told every female pupil the same. Boys were told, engineering or military service if they showed no academic ability. Those who were academic were pointed in the direction of finding a niche career in the local council offices.

Ironically it was the death of Becky's grandfather that put her in a position where she ended up in a bank putting good use to her ability to understand figures.

"Did you always want to be a policeman?"

The smile broke across Colin's face as bright as the sunrise on a summer's morning.

"Ah Becky, that's a long story."

***

"That is an awfully long story," Mother admitted, in response to a question Patricia had asked. The question had been a simple one, 'How did you find Becky, your personal assistant?' The inquiry was borne out of jealousy more than interest. Mrs Fitzgerald would have loved to have her very own personal assistant, but she could not afford such a luxury. The income from the garden barely covered the cost of staff needed to operate the business and left scarcely enough for her to live on. It was true that her divorce settlement was generous, but hiring a personal assistant was not in the budget.

This hint of jealousy Mother easily picked up on. Patricia had always been envious of what other people had. The problem for Mother was admitting that her wayward son had chosen Becky as the family accountant, no doubt considering her legs in the first instance and not her natural ability to handle matters of taxation and investments. Mother's rapier-like mind, even at her age, was still a weapon to be wary of. The long story was modified and adjusted in a moment.

"Becky worked at a high street bank, coincidentally where I had one of my investment accounts."

"Don't you bank at Coutts?"

"I of course do, the majority of my funds are with that dear institution, but it is always wise to support some of the other high street banks, helps competition you know. As I was saying, Becky was working there and so after my illness she had to pop to my home with papers that needed signing, all very boring.

"I must have looked a sight as you can imagine, just over a major heart issue, a table full of pill bottles and Martin nowhere to be seen as usual. Presumably, he was off investigating somewhere. Becky was simply an angel, getting me sorted, helping me unpack, making me a meal. Just being exceptionally kind.

"It turns out she had come from a broken home, looked after by Grandfather, who she in turned cared for prior to his death. Such a sad story. No family, poor girl.

"I, of course, could see there would be a mutual interest in my offering her a job, which she accepted in an instant. The great thing about her is she is so good with figures;

well, she would be working at a bank. She now tends to my financial affairs as well as helping me domestically, a very economical solution I can assure you."

"You are so charitable. I am green with envy, I just have Tamara, my live-in help, sweet Polish girl who can cook and clean, but that is her limit. You mentioned your son Martin, how is his business doing? I heard through the network that he is a private investigator, sounds terribly exciting."

Lunch today was proving to be a good workout for Mother's presentation of 'my life in a positive light' skills. Something that she had not had to rely on in years, having remained within her close social circle of friends. She was enjoying the challenge, however explaining Martin's situation would require a more adept approach. Using the consumption of a tuna and cucumber sandwich as a time-out, Mother constructed her story.

She began with Martin working for the family firm, before touching on his broken engagement and leaving the family business. Most of which she was sure Patricia already knew but wanted to hear again of the Hayden's having a tough time. Then it was onto the business, a detective agency dealing with high class clients and blue-chip companies. She emphasised that Martin was keen to be hands on and keep the agency small, hence he only employed one other person. She also added that Martin was not averse to helping ordinary people who could not possibly afford his daily rates. In the end, Hayden Investigations sounded very much like a cross between a humanitarian organisation and MI5.

Mother added, by way of moving the conversation onto the true purpose of her visit, "I hear Ignatius is now a member of Parliament."

"To be honest I was surprised when he told me."

***

"I was surprised when she said yes," Becky admitted. "I had suggested it, not thinking for one moment she would agree to a weekend away."

"I think you're good for her; she likes to be fussed over and you like fussing over old people. I know Martin cares for his mum; it's just he doesn't know how to show it. I blame his public schooling for bringing men up to be unfeeling. In this life you must be a caring human first, and a gender second."

As much as Becky appreciated Colin's kind comments, she wondered if being considerate to Mrs Hayden when she had first met her, newly discharged from hospital, sent all the wrong messages to the old lady. Becky could not deny that after being made redundant from the bank, Martin offering her the role of family accountant was an opportunity that she would have been a fool to refuse. He was planning to pay her as much as she was getting at the bank, having assured her that he was saving more than enough compared to what his old stick-in-the-mud accountant was charging. But she had imagined, and Martin was of a similar mindset, that she would need to spend one maybe two full days a week on the accounts to keep on top of them. Then there would be the end of year round-up for the taxman to see what he could pick off the bones of the Hayden fortune.

With more free time during the week, Becky was planning to take more accountancy exams, which would put her in a position to open her own company. That was something that she had dreamed of, yet never imagined she could do. The bookkeeping was the easy bit, it was the other business-related chores that she would struggle with, being, as Susan often put it in a friendly jibe, 'off with the butterflies'. Becky knew that her mind was woolly unless there were figures involved. But now, Martin's mother seemed to have grabbed her for daily interaction and Becky being Becky, she was not sure how to say, 'I would rather just be your accountant, not your full-time domestic.'

Yes, Becky had agreed to help Mother convalesce, it was just that she had thought it would only be for a couple of weeks.

"I might be a soft touch Colin, it's just that I have the feeling that Martin's mother has got the taste for gallivanting around, something she no doubt did in her younger years."

"Well look at it this way, if she wants to drag you around the country, all expenses paid, there are a lot worse jobs around."

"Don't look so smug Colin, we'll need a driver don't forget!"

"A wonderful idea but..."

***

"What a wonderful idea, but..." Mother replied, trying to hold in her emotions. She had so far been extremely controlled as she listened to Patricia harp on about her wonderful son. Apart from being an MP, he was also on an important committee that was often shown on television. He apparently got to question all kinds of very important people. He also had been tipped to be an undersecretary in the next reshuffle, which Patricia was assured was now only a matter of weeks away. If that was not bad enough,

Ignatius had promoted a campaign in Grantham to have a statue of Margaret Thatcher erected in recognition of her contribution to the country. It got worse for Mother. The sculpture had already been completed and works were taking place to prepare the site in the centre of Grantham.

Now most people would have been pleased to hear that the battle they had been expecting had already been won. A victory without a cross word being spoken. Mother was not most people. The last thing she wanted to do was admit to Patricia that she had had the same idea. Mother did not like being the last one to arrive at the dinner table.

"...but aren't statues now out of favour, being pulled down and defaced?"

"Well, admittedly there has been a lot of opposition to the project, obviously from all those madcap socialists. But there will be cameras all around the bronze sculpture to deter any vandals."

"Patricia, currently I would have thought Ignatius would have been more adventurous in his visions. Stone effigies of those who have contributed towards society was all right back in the Victorian era. But what do they say about the person, a name, a hint of what they did and nothing else. Apart from obscene graffiti, the only other thing you see on such monuments are bird droppings, which I am sure is not the image we want to see for Mrs Thatcher."

"What would you have done?" Patricia's response was swathed in irritation.

Good question thought Mother. It was not so much a simple inquiry, more a polite way of Patricia saying, 'well if you have a better idea at this late stage, then you had better tell me.' At that exact moment in time Mother had nothing.

All she had was the smallest seed of an idea that germinated into a flower as she began to talk.

"As I said, effigies are nothing more than an empty gesture and a place for tramps to wee and pigeons to poop." She was repeating herself to allow a little breathing space. "We must think of future generations and how to ensure that they are aware of the fine legacy left by the first female prime minister of the United Kingdom." She was still delaying a direct answer, yet the vision was forming and coming into focus.

"We need an education centre," she declared. "A place where anyone, tourists, locals, young and old alike, can visit to learn about the times that she ruled. The mountains that she had to climb. The wars she fought with robust determination and the changes she brought about. Educating future generations is the key, making history available and accessible to all. The shop where she was born should be that place, not a shrine, but a celebration of the lady, the Iron Lady. Now that would make a lot more sense than several hundredweight of bronze stuck on a patch of grass."

It hurt Patricia to think it, but nevertheless she had to accept that it was a good idea. Once she had admitted that fact, it was just a short journey for Mother to insist that she speak to Ignatius at the earliest, that being later in the day, to bring him up to speed with the decision his mother and her friend had made. Conspiring women deciding it would be a triumph for him to announce at the unveiling that he planned to have a Margaret Thatcher centre in Grantham. No doubt this would amass a great many brownie points from his party as well as valuable publicity.

Proudly Mother dug her ancient phone from her bag and called Becky.

"Becky my dear, can we all meet back at the car now? We are going to Grantham."

***

"We are going to Grantham?" Colin repeated what Becky had just told him. "Why are we going back there? This was supposed to be just lunch and then back to the city."

"All she said was we are off to Grantham. She must have blagged a meeting with the MP to beat him into submission over this statue thing she has her heart set on."

Colin wiped his mouth with his cloth napkin and took one last swig of his tea before standing, brushing a few crumbs from his trouser suit. He looked down at Becky and asked her, "Becky, what sort of grey-haired monster have you created?"

Chapter 20

It was a traditional high street straight out of the nineteen-sixties. A two-way road for cars and buses, pedestrians confined to the pavement. There was not even a cycle-lane. As for the shops, just about every one was an independent business. The only concession Grantham had made to modern living was a Costa, a Greggs and a Ladbrokes. All the others were family run, many of which had been established by previous generations.

Now towards the end of the day, the earlier crowds of shoppers were thinning out. Mothers had already collected their children from school and were now at home cooking the evening meal for the family. A few teenagers in school uniform hung around Greggs, lapping up the cut-price sausage rolls and pasties. Fortunately, Martin was able to park right outside Miller Jewellery. Together he and Susan walked into the shop to be greeted by Reggie smiling warmly from the other side of the glass counter.

The single-fronted shop was not big to start with, but even so Mr Miller wanted as much stock on display as possible. His father had told him to do that when he was a small child, many years before he took over the family business. Expensive watches in the stockroom will never sell, so the shop window must be your stockroom. Reggie Miller had stuck to that wise instruction to this day.

Martin and Susan stood in the centre of the shop, which did not have a great deal of room in it. On three sides were glass display cabinets, bright, clean and shiny. To the left were gold rings, bracelets, necklaces, alongside christening gifts, all discreetly lit with small lamps concealed in the frames of the cabinets. On the right was a variety of watches including men's and women's expensive branded ones. On the walls were more glazed cabinets, containing cut glass vases, crystal wine glasses, celebratory champagne flutes, silver picture frames, paperweights and just about anything you might wish to buy as a special gift.

Reggie stood directly in front of them, behind the glass display cabinet dominated by the cash register on the top, as well as the other items required to make the sale, ring gauges, cloths, silver polish, it looked to be his work desk. Behind him, a maroon velvet cloth hung down, no doubt it led to a room at the back.

"Twice in one day Martin. Was this your rendezvous at lunchtime?" Reggie smiled, hoping they had come in to purchase a wedding or engagement ring. He had already noticed the expensive watch that Martin was wearing, and any friend of the Phillips would not be short of a bob or two.

"No, they never turned up. We're here to ask a question which might at first seem strange but trust me it is important. Where around here would I be able to buy a slab of gold?"

"I guess I would need to ask why you would want a slab of gold. If you plan to make your own jewellery, then I can't have you setting up in competition to me," Reggie chuckled. "If you are looking to invest, then you don't want a slab, you would go for a Gold Britannia that the Royal Mint strike, VAT and capital gains free, very popular with investors looking to reduce their tax liability. What's your plan?"

"Making ancient English gold coins," Susan said, trying to keep track of the conversation. All the dazzling gold and diamonds were distracting her.

"Interesting hobby, which I hope is all it is. I'm sure creating English gold coins from any century might be considered illegal. You'd need a bullion dealer, they would sell you the gold, but making coins can be difficult without the correct equipment."

"Do you buy gold in its raw form?"

"You mean just plain gold, yes, I need it when carrying out repairs or alterations, as well as making my own rings, which I enjoy doing. But for that I only need a small furnace to heat the gold to melting point, over a thousand degrees centigrade. To make coins you'll need to make a plaster cast then make a steel master, all before you even think of melting the gold and rolling it. A lot of work for little return unless you are the Royal Mint. Why all the questions, is someone being naughty? I know you are both private eyes."

"We are just trying to get our heads around something," Martin replied cautiously, in the main because he was unsure of exactly what was going on. Luckily Reggie was trying to be helpful.

"If it's old coins you're talking about, the guy you need to speak to is Edwin Stewart, he's the master of that sort of thing. He used to own a shop about four doors away from here. He'll tell you all you need to know. Although rumour has it, he's a little upset that he's not being offered any coins from a recent haul that was found. Has he asked you to find the culprit?"

"Maybe," Martin responded, still trying to understand what Reggie was getting at. Was this haul of rare coins common knowledge throughout the county. He had assumed it was a well-kept secret judging by the way Edwin was planning clandestine meetings in McDonald's.

"If he's not in on the deals, he declares everything to be bogus. You must have heard about the mud he has been slinging at Dave Harvey, shouting out that everything he sells is fake. He's just an angry old man whose time has long since passed."

Susan had to be honest, she was not really paying as much attention as she should have to the dialogue that Reggie and Martin were having. She was mesmerised by a diamond engagement ring. In fact, there were three diamonds on the ring, a cushion-cut solitaire and two round diamonds, one on each side. The trio were set on a platinum band. It cost a lot more than Susan earned in a month. The price was irrelevant to her, it was the exquisite beauty of the ring that she was admiring.

"Mr Miller," she was being formal as she was going to ask a cheeky favour, "could I try that ring on?" She pointed to the ring with the three diamonds.

He guessed she was not a serious buyer, they were asking too many questions for that, but even so Reggie was happy to indulge Susan. Walking around to the cabinet, unlocking, and withdrawing the padded cushioned tray containing a number of other equally beautiful rings. It was not a perfect fit, a little too big for Susan's ring finger, but still she splayed her hand out admiring the way the light reflected off the clear stones.

"Why are you trying a ring on?" Martin asked, sounding a little cantankerous, which in fact he was. He was getting fed up with asking questions and not getting any helpful answers. "You're not getting engaged. You don't even have a boyfriend," he added by way of a taunt.

"No but I have high hopes." Susan sang.

"What does that even mean?"

"Come on Martin," Reggie joined the abstract conversation, "you must have heard of the ant who tried to move a rubber tree plant."

"What?" Martin thought he must be in a dream where he was in Grantham talking to strange people, one of whom was Susan. At least that would mean he might wake up shortly in his own bed, with a feeling of relief.

"Get real Martin, haven't you ever heard it?" Susan turned to Reggie who joined her in the rousing chorus of the Frank Sinatra song that had passed Martin by.

"But he's got high hopes, he's got high hopes, he's got high apple pie in the sky hopes!"

Both Reggie and Susan laughed, leaving Martin confused and slightly irritated, as he came to comprehend he was fully awake.

"Reggie, thank you for your help. You have given us some valuable leads. Susan, give the nice man his ring back. We have one more visit to make. We need to speak to Edwin. I am beginning to think I am being taken for a soft touch."

Reluctantly Susan slid the ring off her finger, returned it to the clammy palm of Mr Miller and followed Martin out of the shop and back to his car.

"You can be very tedious at times you know Martin."

"I know I can because I am getting a little pissed off."

"Does your mother know you swear?" Susan commented, surprised at hearing Martin use such colourful language. He ignored her.

"I came up here for a wedding, which overall should be a pleasant, sociable, and relaxing occasion. The wedding and the related festivities have long since passed and I am still sitting in Grantham High Street. Why? Because you took in a stray dog. A nutter thought he was the victim of a mythical god. A local villain wants to resurrect the Roman Empire. The groom's father conducts a charity, and an old man is pissed off because he is not getting in on the act of being offered a gold coin which frankly, I do not care if it is a fake or not. He can't, and I can't spend it so it's worthless as far as I'm concerned."

"Not a happy bunny, are we?"

"No. This ends here. I might have had some respect for the old bloke, but that has eroded away. I am turning on the engine of this car and driving back to see Edwin to tell him why we are not always invited to the party. Then London nonstop. If you want to stay in this odd town with its affinity for gossip, innuendo and scare mongering, you can step out now and I'll see you in due course."

"Martin, this isn't like you," Susan had changed her tone from flippant to a more serious note. "You're normally so laid back, what's got into you?"

Martin banged the dashboard in frustration before shouting, "Nothing!" He turned towards Susan and regretted his outburst, yet still he could not get the anger out of his body. "This whole thing has been a waste of time; can't you see that? People hear that we are private detectives and think oh, I want them to investigate this or investigate that. All we have done for the last two days is follow shadows and unsubstantiated gossip. Stories that would be better suited to a TV soap drama, not infringing on my weekend."

It was the ring, Martin had to admit it to himself. It was the ring on Susan's finger that had made him on the one hand, think this is it, but he could not propose to her in the shop in front of a relative stranger. And proposing was not what he had planned, it was the wrong way to go about things. He was angry at himself. It was too early for rings, but that was exactly what he wanted to happen soon.

***

He stood on the opposite side of the road in full sight without being seen, that was his skill. People walked past never noticing his presence. Since being in the fast-food restaurant, he had put on a pair of heavy-framed glasses and turned his jacket inside out, so it was now a bright red colour, not the navy blue it had been. He was also appearing to type into his mobile phone, when in fact he was videoing Martin's car. The couple in the car appeared to be having an argument, which did surprise him. The man was obviously shouting and hitting the dashboard with the palm of his hand. There was a clear disagreement between the two passengers, yet the girl appeared to be calm, maybe trying to reassure the driver. The man wished he could work out what they were saying but he had no chance of that, even if he had been on the same side of the road which would have been a big risk.

Then a figure caught his eye. A female figure was walking along the pavement towards Martin's car. Was she going to join them? It could make sense. He observed as she came level with the car. He knew the face well, he had seen her a number of times, she was local. But what was she doing here? Then it all began to make sense, he had her with the wrong accomplice. He watched her walk into Reggie's shop. He needed to make one phone call and he would have the whole answer.

***

"Well if you're driving back to London, I'll stay in the car and hope you are in a better mood by the time we get back." Susan turned and looked away from Martin, she saw a woman walk into the jewellers. "Isn't that the dance teacher Tracey?"

Martin started the engine, pulled on his seat belt, and prepared to move off. Susan grabbed his hand as he tried to put the car into first gear.

"So what! She is more than likely giving him extra lessons to make him Fred Astaire on his anniversary. Put your belt on, we're leaving."

Susan's hand remained on Martin's, she felt his pulse and the warmth radiate into her. It felt reassuring to be touching him, feeling his body, albeit just his arm.

"No, wait!" Susan sounded certain, she was moving snippets of conversations around, seeing the connections. Things were coming into partial focus, not totally clear yet, just a sense of possibilities and ideas developing in her mind. "Reggie knew us by sight, he had seen us at the dance hall, but we never spoke to him. His wife would have told him about us following him. At that point he would have known that we were detectives. But if he arrived at McDonald's to sell a gold coin and saw you with the double milkshake, he would have known it was a trap."

"He'd popped in for his lunch. We're leaving."

"That's what he told you. He also advised us about making gold coins, what you might need. Tracey works metal. She told me her father was a blacksmith. She makes her own Celtic jewellery, casting them, engraving them. She also has dies and presses and the sort of skills you need to make coins. Plus, she is connected with Dave Harvey, the same bloke who has rumours about him and fake coins. She's friendly with him."

"I think you are jumping to conclusions," Martin pointed out as he reapplied the handbrake.

"What, about her? She owns a small shop in a small town, takes dance lessons to earn a few extra pounds, yet buys Rodney a brand-new caravan for cash."

"She might have bought it on hire purchase for him, we don't know."

"But we do, or at least I do. When Rodney said she had bought him a caravan and then he dumped her or she dumped him, it doesn't matter which way around, she didn't take it back, or call in the loan, or even get it repossessed. He kept it. No woman lets a man get away with that unless she had paid cash for it in his name. Hence I asked Becky to make a couple of phone calls. Tracey did buy it cash. At the time I thought, well, business must be good. But what if she is making gold coins? She has the skill set."

Martin turned off the engine, understanding that Susan was on a roll, and it would take time to sort out the jumbled thoughts.

"So," Martin enquired, "is it her and Reggie, her and Dave, her, Dave and Reggie, or just her? Who is making the coins? It might make sense if we work that one out first."

"Hmm, her, I think. She's in there buying the gold, then goes home, makes the coins, and then sells them. I never saw her, but again she could have gone to McDonalds waiting to see a buyer with two milkshakes and sees you. Yes, that makes more sense. Tracey is in there now buying the gold from Reggie to make the coins. Reggie was probably just collecting his lunch. She's the one in all this, even to starting the fire."

"But we never saw her. And don't forget you were spying on me at the time."

"Girls can be slippery characters. Let's go in, I bet she's buying some gold to make the coins."

Without waiting for an answer, Susan exited the car, quickly followed by Martin. Together they went back into the jewellers, not sure what to expect or what the plan might be.

***

"But isn't it a good thing that there's going to be a statue to Margaret Thatcher?" Becky innocently asked as Colin sped north on the A1 towards Grantham.

"Yes, it is good Becky," Mother replied from the luxury of her leather seat in the back of the car, making full use of the drop-down armrest. "But not as good as it could, or should be."

Not one to shy away from a good debate, Colin chimed into the fray. "Wasn't the purpose of this lunch visit to secure an appointment with the Grantham MP to start the process of getting a statue, which as I understand is going to happen, rendering this appointment meaningless?"

"Colleen you might be a good driver, although I am not qualified to judge that as I have never driven. However you do not appear to understand the process of making a difference. Or in fact building on foundations that are already there. True there will be an effigy to the great lady in due course. What I am now planning to achieve is a bigger, more useful, educational facility, which will enlighten future generations as to what she achieved. I do not intend to leave her legacy to a few socialists that will use her statue as a focal point to denounce the policies of future Tory governments. Now just drive."

Which is exactly what he did as swiftly as he could through the rush hour traffic. It was getting late and all three had planned to be back in their own beds before the midnight hour struck.

Chapter 21

They stepped confidently into the shop, which was empty of shopkeeper or dance teacher. Then, alerted by the tinkle of the bell when the door opened, Reggie appeared from behind the velvet curtain. He smiled, appeared happy to see them both so soon after their last visit.

"Tell me you have come back to buy the young lady that ring she so admired."

"What's Tracey doing here?" Susan asked without any formalities, she wanted to get an answer quickly.

"Going to give me a little extra training on the quickstep, heaven knows I need it."

"I wouldn't have thought there was enough room for you to dance the light fandango in here, this is only a small shop," Martin pointed out the obvious. Even he could recall that the quickstep did exactly what it said on the box and needed a lot of space to make it work properly.

"It's all about the hold, the frame, they're just as important as the steps you know." The words were defensive, Reggie was beginning to appear uncomfortable with them in his shop asking questions.

"Can we ask her personally?" Susan moved closer to the counter trying to peer beyond the chinks at the edge of the loose curtain.

"I can't see why not; we have nothing to hide." He pulled back the drape. "Tracey some people want to see you. Go on through." With a smile, he ushered Martin and Susan past the curtain to the stockroom at the back. Susan noticed his hand appeared to be trembling slightly. She then recalled what she had heard in the spa, sweat glands from your fight or flight (sympathetic) nervous system gives you clammy hands. His hands had been clammy when she handed back the ring. She felt the hairs on the back of her neck stand up.

Here in the private part of the shop it was equally as crammed as the front, although not as clean or tidy. A small window high on the back wall filtered a minimal amount of light in. With three people in it, the room was claustrophobic.

Tracey greeted them from a small tatty wooden desk, where she leaned, relaxed and obviously comfortable. Above the desk on the left-hand wall were shelves filled with box files, folders and all manner of detritus that was required to run a sole trader business. On the desk, along with a grey box in front of Tracey, there was an electric kettle, cups, tea and coffeemaking paraphernalia, all squeezed carefully into one corner.

The back wall, under the small porthole of a window, was a work bench littered with the tools of a jeweller, small concise instruments, velvet cleaning cloths and a large desk lamp, currently turned off.

The right-hand wall was free of anything. Little else could be fitted in the room without precluding any humans. There was a safe, but it was not big, it reminded Susan of the one in the office when she worked for an accounts department. It was only waist high, but solid looking and ancient. It had been handed down from father to son and now would be little more than a locked cabinet to a modern safe cracker.

"What can I do for you two?" Tracey asked, having closed the grey box in front of her.

"We heard a nasty rumour concerning you today," Susan began. "About you starting a fire at your ex-boyfriend's house. Can't be true, can it?" The question was rhetorical, but Tracey was happy to answer.

"I might have started it if I could have been sure that he was there and would have died in the conflagration. But he wasn't and I didn't."

"But you were seen starting the fire at Rodney's," Martin added.

"Ah, you must have been talking to that old slag Vera. When Rodney told me that Vera had blamed me for burning the house down, I simply pointed out to him that it would be her word against mine. I run an established well-respected business in Grantham as well as holding dance classes. My word, or that of a dope-smoking pensioner who lays on her back at the drop of a hat. The truth is I never started that fire. I told him to look towards his OAP bed partner." Her normally soft voice was full of malice and bitterness.

"Is that why Rodney blamed Jupiter for the fire, to keep you out of the picture?" Susan was beginning to think that Tracey was being a little too defensive.

"More like keeping his bit on the side safe."

"Or was it?" This time Martin weighed in with his theory of the situation. Vera might be a lot of things, but he could never see her being vindictive or destructive. If things were not working out with Rodney she would have moved on, or even shared him. "You reminded Rodney that if he pointed the finger at you, you would point the finger at him drug dealing on the bus with Vera."

Tracey chuckled, the thought of drug dealing amongst pensioners on a bus always made her laugh, it was one of those unbelievable situations that she could never have imagined had she not seen it for herself. "All very amusing but I'm having some jewellery valued, so if you don't mind go about your business and leave us innocent people in peace."

"Not dance lessons then?" Susan pointed out. Tracey looked at Reggie who stood mostly in the shop, holding the curtain back, Tracey's eyes betrayed the lie that she had inadvertently exposed.

"Maybe later."

Before anyone else could speak, the high-pitched doorbell tinkled alerting them that a customer had entered the shop. Reggie turned to serve the customer, pulling the curtain closed behind him.

"What do you know about old gold coins from the reign of Henry VI?" Martin asked.

"Nothing, but I sense you are going to contradict me."

"Well, the book all about medieval coins was found in Rodney's bedroom. I doubt it belonged to him and most certainly has never belonged to Vera. Must have been yours, something you left behind when collecting your belongings."

Still sitting at the table, Tracey looked up at both Martin and Susan, she shook her head, a slight movement that continued as she spoke.

"I have no idea what you two are investigating, but I do get the sense that you want to find me guilty of something. Can I suggest that we save ourselves a lot of time and you just accuse me? I will deny it and then we can go about our business. What is it I am meant to have done?"

"You are producing fake gold coins as well as bogus Roman coins." Susan as ever was not shy at coming forward.

"Am I really? Can I suggest you both leave it there, walk away. Otherwise, I will want to speak to you with my lawyer present who will be suing you for slander."

It sounded like a bluff to Martin, he hoped it was, as the last thing he wanted now was a summons to court, his mother would not approve. However, he did still have something in his armoury.

"Didn't someone, not drug-induced Vera, say to me that each Sunday you get a lift from Dave Harvey after your dance class. If fact even I saw you get in his car once. It was common knowledge." Martin wanted to push the blade in deep, he felt sure now was the time. "Then Rodney's house, where I was also told you had a room full of boxes and things and that Rodney never knew what was in them. But Vera did tell me, on one of her voyages of discovery, that one of those boxes in your room was full of old funny looking coins, a bit like this one here." Martin held the small Roman coin in his fingers to make sure she could see it. "Fortunately, those boxes were moved out the day before the fire started, maybe that was when you dropped this one. I would also add that I know Dave Harvey brings all his new stock into the church on Monday for staff to sort and list. It might only be a dot-to-dot puzzle in my mind, but I am seeing a clear picture starting to form. Maybe the contents of that box in front of you might help to answer a few of my questions."

It was an uncomfortable silence, the three of them staring at each other, waiting for one to speak, in the end it was none of them. Reggie spoke from behind Martin and Susan.

"Sounds like these gumshoes are going to be a thorn in our side."

Susan turned to look at Reggie while Martin continued to stare at Tracey.

"Martin," Susan sounded unusually timid, "you should look at this."

Martin turned around, he did not like what he saw. He had seen firearms before, but he had never had a pistol aimed at him in a threatening way. It was a neat compact gun which looked unreal as it pointed towards him. He was captivated by the weapon. It had a semi-matt finish, a short compact barrel. He could imagine that as the trigger was pressed, the top would flip up and a flame would appear. He recalled such a cigarette lighter when he was young, a novelty. He doubted that this one would light any cigarette, instead it would put a nasty hole in your chest.

The next part of the conversation between Tracey and Reggie was in Martin's view a little ordinary, considering the gun in Reggie's hand. Tracey was surprised that Reggie owned a gun, let alone was prepared to point it at anyone. She even questioned if it was loaded or not, which is not the best sort of conversation to have in front of the two people you are intimidating with the aforesaid weapon.

Reggie confirmed it was indeed loaded. The gun originally belonged to his father who like Reggie kept it as a form of insurance against robbers who might consider using a lesser lethal weapon, such as a cosh or a baseball bat. The gun outtrumped those effortlessly. The only word of wisdom Reggie's father gave him in terms of self-defence of the shop's valuable stock, was if the raider had a gun, give him everything and leave your gun out of sight because you are not going to win a fast draw situation. So, the gun had been unable to fully insure against theft, but Reggie was making use of it now.

"The two of you, sit on the floor next to the safe, and sit on your hands." Reggie flicked the gun in the direction of the safe, neither Martin nor Susan needed precise instructions, they could see the safe. Reluctantly, they sat on their hands, the cold concrete floor adding to their discomfort as they awaited what Reggie planned for them.

Martin was glad to sit down next to the safe on his hands, for no better reason than he felt his legs begin to shake and he doubted they would hold his weight much longer with a gun pointing at him. Susan was next to him, looking as defiant as ever. He wondered if she had ever had a gun aimed at her in anger. He did not recall her ever saying she had, but he was confident that Susan, always one to share stories of her life, would have mentioned it had it occurred.

He clearly understood that they were both in danger, which was not exactly rocket science. But this was potentially life-threatening, real danger, nothing close to a fight where you get punched, maybe get a split lip. Nor the danger from crashing into another car, where the car blows up its air cushions and protects you. This was real danger. Death might only be the click of a trigger away. In that moment of fear, Martin regretted that Susan had not shared his stars for the day, they might have forewarned him. Not that he would have heeded any of her words, but perhaps he might do in the future if he had a future to look forward to.

"It was you who came to McDonald's to sell gold coins." Martin had assumed that the term gumshoe was in the main obsolete, but hearing Reggie use the term made him aware that it was more common than he had at first thought.

"I will admit I was surprised to see you sitting there with your two milkshakes. It did throw me at first, but I quickly purchased some food and thought I had best talk to you, just in case you had seen me come in. It would not have done for you to see me walk in then walk straight back out again, that would have given the game away. I presume it was old man Edwin who sent you. The supposed buyer from Manchester sounded very keen to see my goods. Is Edwin still annoyed that he has not been offered anything?"

"I would say that was the case," Martin replied. Already his hands felt as if they were going to sleep. "But I daresay flogging a fake gold coin so near to home might be dangerous."

This time it was Tracey, now standing up, who looked down at the couple and answered, "Who said they are fakes? You must have heard the story of the hoard discovered in Lincolnshire, the finder not wanting to share the proceeds with the landowner. Everyone, especially coin collectors, love a bargain, particularly an under the counter one. That gave us the perfect cover story for the coins sudden appearance."

Changing the subject, Susan spoke, her voice now strong and defiant, if there was going to be a fight, Susan was up for it. It was just the only times she had been caught up in brawls were after a night's drinking, never this early in the day. "It takes a lot of money to buy a boyfriend a caravan for cash, something you have done. In the same way you have everything required to produce coins from the Roman Empire, using your smithy skills, dies, heat and an artist's talent in creating complex designs. You also have a dark streak in you, burning down your ex-boyfriend's house is not the normal reaction to breaking up. I've broken up with loads of boyfriends, not burned down any houses yet."

Martin continued offering evidence too, albeit circumstantial, he was happy to point the finger. "Selling cheap denarius is something Dave Harvey does, but he is shy about exactly where his supplies come from. Then there is the amazing discovery of a hoard of King Henry's coins found in Lincolnshire, yet not offered to one of the foremost collectors of coins in the county. Maybe that would have sparked a lot of questions that you now need to answer."

"You are both still making some very wild allegations," Tracey told them.

"But it would not take much to disprove them," Susan replied. "Let's pop along to your workshop, you can show us around, I'm sure any evidence will be there. The production of coins needs certain things as I know you are aware."

"Maybe," Martin spoke looking at the grey box on the desk, "show us what is in that box."

"Let's show them, shall we?" Tracey said to Reggie with a cynical smile.

Without waiting for an answer, Tracey opened the box, took out a wad of tissue paper which she proceeded to unravel, to reveal a small gold coin. She held the coin carefully in front of her for Martin and Susan to see.

"I think this is what you are talking about." Tracey smiled, as she rolled the coin around her fingers. "It is, if I say so myself, an absolute work of art. I doubt even King Henry himself could tell the difference. So far, all our customers have been more than happy. They are also pleased that they were especially singled out to have the chance of one of these special super rare coins.

"It's a peculiar trait that collectors of anything rare: coins, paintings, figurines, pottery, if they acquire a very rare item, they're happy to keep it quiet, not share it with others. I have always thought that a little selfish. But collectors can be odd and very strange at times."

Carefully Tracey put the coin back in the box, explaining it was one from the latest batch she had made for Reggie, her production partner. He acquires the gold through the normal channels raising no suspicion given his business. She then melts it down in her furnace, before using a set of steel casts to form first the plain disc, then by means of a very high-pressure die forms the coin. Not exactly like modern coin production that you might see at the Royal Mint, more like the way they were made back in the times of Henry the Sixth. She returned the box to the desk.

"She's being very modest," Reggie added, again smiling proudly as he looked at Tracey. "It takes a very special skill to create such a coin that fools some very knowledgeable collectors. Tracey has a natural ability to create fine works of art, I'm glad we teamed up."

"So you sell a few fake coins, I am sure it is not worth pointing a gun at someone," Martin pressed.

"Oh, that is where you are so wrong." Tracey once again sat down, relaxed that her hostages were under the control of her partner in crime. "As soon as eBay began, I could see a market for coins that appeared to be old yet were not. I have been selling old coins for years: Roman coins, old English coins, even some American coins from the time of the revolution. Susan has seen my skills at producing Celtic bangles and bracelets with their engraved patterns. It's not a big step to create a master die and then produce coins by the thousands."

"You're a habitual forger?" Susan asked, not believing what she heard.

"Proud to say yes to that question. Even Dave Harvey thinks what he gets every week comes from archaeological digs across eastern Europe. Although knowing what Dave is like, making money is his reason for being, so he does not ask too many questions."

"So why gold coins?"

"Look upon it as an expansion of business, a profitable one. When Reggie joined the dance class, I began to think here's a man who can get hold of something I can't. And there are many gold coins that I have thought about creating but was unable to source the raw materials without causing suspicion."

"Hence the King Henry coins."

"No," Reggie joined in the bragging, not wanting to miss out. It was not every day you could tell someone how well you are doing as a criminal. Even his wife had no idea about this side-line. "There are many gold coins in the world that have a higher value than the raw material. Most of them are in fact Roman or Greek, ironic really, selling cheap bronze coins to Dave Harvey to peddle on his website and all the while Tracey is using her skills and my raw materials to produce gold coins that are worth thousands. The best part is once the mould is made, we can churn them out by the hundreds. For example, a gold stater that was struck during the reign of Philip II, Alexander the Great's father, might sell for three grand, we can sell it for two and still make a handsome profit."

"Because it's a fake, that's why you make money. You're doing something illegal," Susan was happy to point out.

For all the boasting, Martin could see that this was not just a couple of locals knocking out a few fakes to earn some pin money. He had earlier Googled the Henry coins and seen that they were worth about seven thousand pounds. The two of them were no doubt making a lot of money from their illegal enterprise. Martin began to wonder just how far they would go to protect their investments. He was fearful about a gun being directed at him. Now, as he listened to his captors, he began to suspect neither he nor Susan would get out of this alive.

"It might be illegal," Reggie acknowledged, the gun held firmly and confidently in his hand, "but we are also providing our customers with a service. They are not complaining that they are being robbed. Everyone is a winner."

"But they are paying for something which is not the genuine article. It's like me going into Debenhams and buying a Gucci handbag, I'd want it to be the real thing."

"Of course you would. But if you bought one off a market trader at half the price, you might expect that it was not the real thing. But would those around you know where you bought it from and could they tell it was a fake. I doubt it. Those coin collectors who buy our wares, are more concerned about how good it looks than how real it is."

"Well as long as everyone is happy, you might as well let us get on our way and toddle back to London, don't you think?" Susan asked, not expecting a positive answer, but if you don't ask you don't get.

"Sadly, you have become a problem to us," Tracey said, this time looking at Reggie.

The last thing Martin wanted to hear was that they were a problem. Of course, you can solve problems in many ways, some easy, some hard. Given the current circumstances and the fact that Susan had already established that jumping back in their car was not going to be an option, he guessed whatever the final choice of action might be, it was not going to benefit either him or Susan.

Casually Reggie sat on the desk beside Tracey without taking his eyes off his captives.

"I'm not going to risk all we have built up, we have far too much to lose and much to gain if they're not able to talk. I have often wondered about such circumstances arising and what I would do. I was more thinking of one person, which would be a simple gunshot in the shop. A simple self-defence during a robbery. Two people, slightly more difficult, but I'm thinking of firing a bullet through one into the other, tragic but still self-defence as they tried to rob me."

"Isn't that a danger, having the police nosing around," Tracey said cautiously. "That was why I persuaded Rodney not to accuse me. I didn't want anyone asking questions, always wondering what they might see or turn up."

"Yes, but a spur of the moment robbery, I thought they had a gun, so I fired in self-defence. The police would not go searching and anyway you can make sure all the coins and gold are at your place. Trust me it will work."

Martin was proved right; the solution was not going to benefit them in the least. Now it was clear their lives were going to be sacrificed to conceal the criminal activity, Martin started to form a plan.

"Susan, what would Jim Rockford do in this situation?" Even at the point of possible violent death, Martin did not want to waste time or energy trying to think of something that had already been mapped out in the TV detective series.

"I don't recall." Susan turned to Reggie. "Anyway, we're not regular villains going around robbing shops, the police will never believe you. He," she nodded towards Martin, "has a load of money so he doesn't need to rob anyone."

Good point, Martin thought but was not sure if it would hold favour. In fact, in the ideas department he had no answer. The minute he moved he would be shot. If he stayed still, he would be shot in the fullness of time, but at least that might give Susan more chance of coming up with a better plan.

Weirdly, as Martin began to think about dying, he was pleased that he was sitting beside Susan who was going to suffer the same fate. He recalled the words that Colin had spoken about relationships always ending up in tears as one partner dies, at least they would die together. He would not have to suffer the pain of losing her and he wished that she would feel the same way about losing him. The fact that Susan was next to him was going to make death a lot easier to face. He would have liked to squeeze her hand, but he was sure that was not an approved movement.

"If you are sure?" Tracey sounded hesitant.

"I'll shoot them. You help me move the bodies into the shop then you get off home and you need never be part of it." Reggie, the once timid sounding husband, seemed more like a hitman for the mafia, having a clear plan in his mind.

"Let's get this done then." Tracey was now resigned to what was about to happen.

"It'll never work, we have no motive," Susan shouted, there was a tone of alarm in her voice.

"Shut up." Reggie stood up. "Listen carefully, I will say this only once."

Martin wanted to point out that the expression he was using was from an old TV comedy series, the name of which he could not at that moment recall. He wondered if this might be some prank his mad rugby players might be playing on him, he hoped so.

Reggie continued with his instructions. "Both of you stand up slowly, very slowly, be warned I have a very nervous trigger finger. Susan, hold your hands out to the side so I can see them clearly, then Martin, stand in front of Susan."

They followed the instructions slowly and precisely. Martin wondered what would happen if he dived for the gun, he could not be sure never having carried out such an action before.

"Now Susan put your arms around Martin and cling to him tightly. I want to ensure the bullet travels cleanly through you both."

"I am not putting my arms around Martin just because you want me to," Susan complained loudly, for no better reason than she did recall that Jim Rockford always tried to delay getting shot, to either allow time to be rescued or an advert break to be screened. Her loud voice drowned out the high-pitched tinkle of the doorbell, no one realised a customer had entered the shop.

A second later the curtain was swung open widely, sunlight from the shop flooding the back room. They all turned to see who was standing there. Martin recognised the figure at once.

"What on earth are you doing here?" Martin shouted.

Chapter 22

If you need to have an uncomfortable conversation with someone and want to conclude it without fear of interruption or distraction, then the interior of a moving vehicle is as good a place as any. The dialogue that Becky wanted to have with Mother was a simple one, yet Becky guessed it might be difficult to win Mother around to her point of view.

On the evidence of the last three days Becky concluded that Mother was fighting fit again and had no need of anyone to look after her. How you tell the person you have been cooking and cleaning for over the last few weeks, that that is the end of their free ride, Becky was not sure. In the end she decided to take Colin's advice, be blunt, be bloody-minded, be stubborn.

"Mrs Hayden, after today I think it's time I went back to my accounting duties," Becky did not sound bold, nor bloody-minded and certainly not stubborn. Colin turned and looked at her with a grin that said, one nil to Mother already.

"I do hope you have not been neglecting your duties with regard to our finances, that would be very remiss of you, considering we are paying you not an insubstantial amount."

"No," Becky indignantly corrected her, "I have carried out my duties in that respect. I am talking about the additional tasks."

"Such as?" Mother asked.

"Well, looking after you mainly."

"And that is very kind and considerate of you. Such a wonderful example of the younger generation supporting the senior. I am truly grateful and thankful I have such a steadfast hand to adhere to my own frail one."

"Not going well is it?" Colin commented with a big smile on his face.

"Shut up," Becky replied in a low tone of voice before raising her volume over the road noise to tell Mother like it was, or at least try to.

"But that's not what I am employed to do."

"That makes it an even greater sacrifice you are making to help look after a delicate old lady."

"I am only employed part-time so that I can have more time to plan for my future."

"Well, my dear, how hard can it be to get married and have a family, everyone does that."

As much as Colin was enjoying this entertaining conversation between Becky and a battling old lady, who was clearly on the winning side of the argument, Colin decided it was only fair to put in his own two pennyworth, something he was never afraid to do.

"First," Colin started, "not everyone wants to get married and have a family. Secondly, I would never have described you as a delicate old lady, far from it. What Becky is trying to say is that she will not be looking after you in the future, you will have to cook, clean and wipe your own arse as Becky will be looking after the household coffers in such an efficient way that you could always employ a real nurse to look after you. And before you ask, I am driving this car as a favour to Becky, not to you. After tonight I will go back to my day job of being a fashion icon. Becky will go back to looking after your accounts and planning for her own future. And you will need to rekindle your independence."

It was not often that Mother was lost for words. She had been left speechless when as a young teenage girl a rather crabby old man leered at her. He followed up with some very improper comments about her body. Mother was not so much speechless then but more outraged. In place of words, she pushed her clenched fist with some significant force into the old man's nose, causing it to bleed and for him to retreat to which ever stone he had emerged from.

Today she was not exactly speechless but not in a position to punch Colin on the nose, although part of her wanted to. Instead, she simply said, "Well if that's the way Becky feels."

There was a silence between the trio, an uncomfortable tense one that might have lasted for many hours had Mother not decided that she needed these two to be at least civil with her over the next few hours. Otherwise seeing how cantankerous Colin could be, she might find herself without a driver or even worse, left at the side of the road.

"Becky dear, what plans do you have for the future?" Mother sounded contrite, an occasion which occurred with the same frequency as Halley's Comet.

Turning in her seat to face Mother, Becky began to explain how she planned to continue studying accountancy and take her exams, hopefully passing them within a couple of years. Then she would set about getting a few years' experience in a commercial setting before branching out on her own to set up Hunter Accounts. She had always dreamed of her name in lights and that was about as close as she would get.

The olive branch that Mother had offered worked and as Colin drove slowly along the street looking for the location of Ignatius Fitzgerald's office, Becky and Mother were laughing like best friends.

The MP's office was a simple shop front set on the High Street with a large poster picture of Ignatius, his name in large lettering appeared on the shop façade. Across the window, superimposed at the top of this slightly creepy portrait, were the words, 'Member of Parliament for Kesteven', followed by the subheading, 'Making Grantham Great.'

In Colin's judgement, it was a carbuncle on the High Street, no doubt pushing out valuable retail outlets, which provided both a good service and value for money; he doubted those were on offer in an MP's shop.

What he had seen on the opposite side of the road to where he had finally parked, was Martin's car, outside Miller's Jewellery. As he recalled Miller was the surname of the barmaid, who had mentioned that her husband was a jeweller.

"Looks like your son is working hard. Either that or buying a ring and getting engaged," he joked not realising that such a topic was non-grata in Mother's mind.

All three got out of their car and stood on the pavement looking at Martin's, wondering just why it might be there.

"What makes you think he is getting engaged?" Mother asked, trying to sound as calm as she could.

"Come on, you said yourself everyone wants to get married sometime," Colin reminded her.

"That would be so nice." Becky added, "I think they'd make a lovely couple."

"That might be so," Mother concluded, "but he is not going to get engaged or married without asking me first." Once again, she was in a fighting mood. Maggie's education centre was put to one side for the moment and Mother stormed across the road and burst into the shop.

"Shouldn't we stop her?" Becky asked.

"No, I'm sure he's not buying a ring. If he was going to buy one for his future wife, it would be Mappin and Webb not Miller's Jewellery of Grantham."

***

The arrival of his mother into the centre of the predicament threw Martin for a split second, as it did Susan, who had her arms tightly around him. The captors also wondered just why an old lady had pushed her way into the back room of the shop at such an impractical moment.

"Who are you?" Tracey asked, sounding surprised.

"The question should be who are you and what are you doing to my son? Susan are you being forced to...?" Mother began.

He might have been distracted for a split second, but Martin could see this was going to be the only opportunity to turn the tables. He would have liked to have been polite and first ask Mother just what she was doing here and why she had come into the shop putting herself in danger.

Instead, he dived forward, lunging at Reggie, grabbing his wrists, trying to wrench the gun from his hand. At the same time, Susan got stuck into Tracey. It was not the first time that Susan had been in a woman-to-woman brawl, so she knew a few tricks and punches that would weaken her stronger adversary. Seconds later, they were on the floor, rolling and pulling at each other.

At the same time Martin was wrestling with Reggie in the corner of the room against the safe, his leg getting tangled with the two women fighting. Being the younger man, Martin was now getting the upper hand ever so slightly. The gun was away from Reggie which made Martin feel a little more on equal terms.

Over the melee, Mother called out with as strong a voice as she could muster, she was not used to such behaviour. No one had seen her bend down and pick up a discarded item.

"Everyone stop now, or I'll shoot!"

They all did stop, without releasing their grip on their respective opponents, to see Mother standing over them, pointing the gun at no one in particular.

***

"We'd best go across anyway, see if they need help with Mother," Becky decided, knowing Mother was very feisty when it came to anyone talking about Martin and Susan as a couple.

"Suppose you're right," Colin sounded hesitant, "she can be very unpredictable at times."

They stood on the pavement preparing to cross over the road to the shop, when around them everything changed. Cars sped from both the left and the right. Cars with alternating headlights, blue lights flashing and with the noise of heavy braking. From a tranquil market town high street, the road had been transformed into a vortex of activity. Police cars stopping, heavily protected officers with weapons were dashing from their vehicles. Other officers starting to hold back the inquisitive by-standers. A larger police carrier arrived, mounting the pavement and almost colliding with Martin's car. More officers evacuated from the back, joining an ever-increasing line of armed police officers going into the shop.

Mesmerised, Becky watched the activity, which resembled a scene from an action film, she half expected someone to shout, 'cut!' and everyone relax. That did not happen.

Colin observed, impressed with the speed of the process, part of him missed being involved in such operations.

"Let's hope Mother hasn't decided to take up armed robbery to fund her dream of a Maggie Thatcher Centre," Colin commented, then added, "Best check her handbag for weapons in future."

Chapter 23

It was hot and stuffy, with little children running around and screaming. The table was a little sticky and the music was from an earlier decade, of that Martin was convinced. He was also certain that he did not really want to be in this drab, poorly lit carvery that required a major refurbishment. It was not just the building that needed an overhaul, the food could have done with a shot of flavour and the dried-up vegetables should never have seen the light of day, let alone be on his plate.

It was only that the invitation Ken Wilson had given them as he collected them from the police station was hard to refuse, given what he had done for them. Reporters have a habit of being in the right place at the right time. Ken, being a local hack, in addition had a lot of sway with the police that had gathered up the five suspects, one of whom was armed, that they found in the back of the jewellers and marched them all down to the nick.

"I know just the place for a decent bite to eat and a debrief. I bet you have lots of questions, for which I have the answers." He smiled as he drove them out of the police station yard, towards the outskirts of Grantham.

Martin did have plenty of questions. The first he would have liked to ask was, 'if this was decent food Ken, what's your bad food like?' In the end, being the respectful man he was, he just asked, "How come you called the police?"

Ken pushed his plate to one side, having cleared off just about everything on it, just a wide drizzle of thick brown gravy was left. He leaned back on his chair, clasping his hands behind his head, then smiled triumphantly. Ken liked to recount his adventures to anyone who would listen, especially successful escapades.

"It's a bit of a long story; hence it would be better if I start at the beginning."

After meeting Martin and Susan in the betting shop, Ken realised that their questions were the same ones that he had been grappling with over the last couple of years. There were constant rumours that Dave Harvey was selling fake Roman coins, it was just identifying where he was obtaining them from which was proving difficult. Tracey was always the prime suspect in the conspiracy. She had the required skills and was on good terms with Dave Harvey, but the police, Ken knew, were not keen to act unless they had concrete evidence against him. He decided to put the whole story on the backburner until Martin and Susan appeared to be looking at the fake coin story with fresh eyes.

Since the moment Martin left the hotel that morning, Ken had followed him as well as Susan after she had joined her boss, co-director, Susan quickly corrected him.

In the hope the pair might turn up something new, Ken sat in McDonald's watching Martin who was clearly waiting for someone who did not turn up. Then they were off to the dark side of town, not the normal surroundings sightseers to Grantham would visit. Now Ken was really thinking the London duo had found out something interesting. When they parked outside the jewellers, Ken still had no idea what they were up to. But his nose for a story was twitching like mad, so he just knew deep down something was afoot.

Then he saw Tracey walk into the shop. That was the moment he started to connect the dots. Seeing her had reminded him of the other man in McDonald's who he half recognised but could not place. Then it came to him, at the dance class, that was where he had seen the fellow who spoke to Martin. Was this a new connection? Ken could not be sure. Instead, he called the local coin expert, Edwin. The question he asked was a simple one, 'Were any of the fake coins that we all assumed Dave was selling, silver?'

It was then that Edwin told Ken that there were now gold coins being faked. Proudly telling the reporter he knew that Martin, a private investigator, was on the case.

Ken took Dave out of the equation and replaced him with the jeweller, Reggie. This made so much more sense. Tracey and Reggie working together could pass coins onto Dave, who no doubt did not ask too many questions. That was why there was never any real evidence against him.

Ken then walked past the shop to see what was going on. He saw no one in it. This either meant Martin and Susan were in cahoots, which he doubted, or something was amiss. Ken stepped into the shop to see first-hand what was going on. As he walked in, he sensed he caught Reggie, who had just emerged from the back room through the curtain, doing something he should not. Ken caught a fleeting glimpse of Susan in the back room. If that was not bad enough, he also noticed Reggie putting something down behind the counter out of view of the person who had just walked in. Ken was convinced it was a gun. He asked a question about a nearby road, received directions from Reggie and left. The reporter was shy of being anywhere near a gun of any description.

"It was at that point I called the police and said I suspected an armed robbery was taking place at the shop. Then I saw an old lady go in."

Not sure what else he should do, he just watched as a few moments later the police arrived in force.

"And arrested all of us," Susan pointed out, having been handcuffed and dragged into a waiting police van.

"Well, they had no idea at that moment who the good guys were. I think finding an old lady waving a gun around was a bit of a surprise to them."

"Thankfully," Martin replied, "they just walked her to the car, she didn't realise that she was under arrest or else there might have been some fireworks."

In the chaos back at the police station, it was Ken who used his influence to point the police in the right direction. The gold coins in the back room were a strong clue. Then, once the police searched Tracey's flat and shop, it became obvious that she was at the heart of a counterfeiting ring. Reggie tried to deny it but soon backed down. Their combined charge sheet would have a long list of illegal activities.

"I was told off the record by the police," Ken admitted, "that the two of them appear to have a bit of a counterfeit empire going on, a very lucrative one, which is no doubt the reason they were prepared to kill to protect it."

"Well, we certainly have a lot to thank you for," Martin spoke graciously. "In particular for getting the police to agree to let my mother make her statement at a London police station in the morning."

"Martin could not stand another night in a hotel with his mother," Susan joked.

"Susan, that's not true. I just don't want her wearing herself out."

As for the statements that Susan and Martin needed to make, they were resigned to spending most of the next day in the police station giving their version of events. Consequently, they were to have another night in a hotel.

"Henry Phillips called to tell me that you have had a word with him about his activities. You can see now why it must all be kept discreet."

"Yes indeed. The one thing that does concern me is that Vera will be interviewed as a witness by the police over the fire at Rodney's house. Will she end up in court over her own business activities?" Martin was concerned because however weird and disagreeable Vera might be, he did not want to see her in prison. That would not seem to be fair, but he acknowledged the law is the law and once the police heard about her BPB gang, it would probably not end well for her.

"Ah, Vera and her bus trips." Ken laughed, finished his lager top and dramatically banged the glass down on the table for no reason. "The police are fully aware of what she is up to, but there are bigger fish to fry out there. With only limited police resources available, they ignore her. She does little harm and in some instances, helps older people that buy her gear for their pain. She'll give a statement about the fire and that will be that. She'll be back on the bus the same day."

"Does that mean that Rodney gets his insurance pay out?" Susan asked.

"I guess he might as long as Tracey admits to starting the fire, then the insurance company will have to pay out. What Rodney will do with the money is anyone's guess. Knowing him, as I do, he'll more than likely stay in the caravan and invest the money in some dreamt-up business that will see it all frittered away. Being a gambling man, I would bet one hundred pounds, that if you both come back in five years, you'll find Rodney in the caravan, still driving buses and almost penniless."

Martin had no plans to return to Grantham ever. It did not occur to him that he would need to return in the fullness of time to stand in the witness box when Reggie and Tracey were put on trial. For now, he was happy for Ken to take them back to the jewellers to collect his car.

***

It was not late, yet both Martin and Susan, sitting in the bar nursing their drinks, felt totally exhausted. It had been a day they never expected to face in their entire lives and never wanted to face again. Now with just the two of them together, it was time to reflect.

"I still don't understand why Tracey started going out with Rodney in the first place. Her talking about mothering him just doesn't hold water for me."

"Unless we ask her, maybe we'll never know, but I have a theory. She wanted somewhere close to the temple to store her illegal goods. She was simply using him. In the end though, she must have had some feelings for him as she did burn down the house after catching him with Vera. Speaking as a man I know how complex women's minds can be at times," Martin laughed.

"Talking of complex, you do realise Martin, that your mother most likely saved our lives by stepping through that curtain at that moment. It would make a great episode for the Rockford Files. It just scares me how close we were to being murdered."

"I do hope," Martin held onto Susan's hand, "that you will not be mentioning that to Mother. If you do, I will never hear the last of it."

Susan smiled, finished her drink and indicated to a waiter to bring her a refill.

"Thankfully the cavalry arrived in time," Martin added, joining Susan with another gin and tonic.

"And how brave were you Martin Hayden. Who'd have thought you'd launch yourself at a gunman and succeed in disarming him."

Yes, who would have thought it. Not Martin that was for sure. It was one of those actions that you do instinctively. With Reggie not looking at him, it was the only opportunity he was going to get. There just was not time to balance up the pros and cons. He was going to die anyway, so if Reggie had turned to see him lunging at him and fired, he would have only missed out on a few minutes of life.

It was strange, he had never thought about dying before sitting on that cold floor with a gun pointed at his head. Death was decades off. When he was as old as his mother then he might start thinking about dying and begin to accept the inevitable.

Yet as he stood in front of Reggie, Susan clinging onto him, he did not mind facing death and was ready to accept it. He'd had a good life, albeit a short one, and if he was to die alongside anyone, he was glad it was Susan sharing the moment. Warmly he told her, "I've learnt with you beside me that I can deal with almost anything. With you next to me I felt no fear, not even facing the prospect of death."

"Ah, that's really sweet of you Martin. Does that mean you'll be less grumpy when I make a fool of myself?"

"I can't promise you that, and I still want to turn a deaf ear when you tell me my horoscope. But I wouldn't change you."

"That's good, 'cause your stars were really weird today. It mentioned something about starting a new career, which I guess might have been the case had you been shot and killed. You'd have a new career as an angel, or a devil, not sure which," Susan joked, before her voice took on a serious tone. "Like you, I was glad you were next to me, I felt safe and confident you'd find a way out."

Martin had hesitated yesterday over dinner. He wanted to ask Susan for a date but could not find the right words and in the end, her telephone had interrupted him and kicked the moment into touch. If he had died today, she would never have known just how he felt about her. The words he planned might not be the best, but as long as they conveyed the sentiment they would have to do. Martin finished his drink and looked into Susan's grey-green eyes. He took a deep breath and spoke,

"Susan, I'm not sure how to put this, it is something I have been wanting to ask you, but just have not found the right time if there ever is such a thing. Tomorrow, we spend the day here giving our statements to the police. With a bit of luck and a following wind we will be back in our own beds tomorrow night. Let's have a couple of days off, recharge our batteries and then on Friday night, I want to take you out for a meal."

"That'd be nice Martin, give me a chance to catch up on my washing and stuff. Where shall we go, somewhere posh on the company credit card?"

"No, the company is not paying for it, I am, because I am taking you out. Martin Hayden wants to take Susan Morris out, not Susan the employee, not Susan the director. I want to take Susan Morris the woman out on a date, which if I am being honest is long overdue."

"A date? A real date?"

"Yes. It will be nothing like any previous first dates you have had as we know each other well enough already. But between the two of us I hope it works out. One thing today has taught me is that staying alive does not come with a written guarantee, you must live your life while you have it, make every moment count. What do you say? Friday night date?"

"Wow!"

Author Notes

I hope that you enjoyed the latest episode in Martin and Susan's life, I know I enjoyed writing it.

I should point out a few things about Grantham. It is not a vortex of drug dealers, forgers, prostitutes and arsonists. Grantham is a very pleasant market town, that I have had the pleasure of visiting on several occasions. It is also the birthplace of Margaret Thatcher. Whatever your opinion of her, she was our first female Prime Minister, hence the town has recognised that fact by way of a statue.

Many of the places mentioned in the book are just figments of my imagination, including the MP and his constituency.

While researching for this book, I found there is a large group of people scattered around the world, who follow the principles and customs of the Roman Empire, happy to dress in the traditional costumes from that period. Weirdly, I attended a carol concert at my local church and there was a Roman Centurion taking part. He clearly took the whole thing very seriously; and his costume to the untrained eye could well have been the real thing.

Now at last Martin has asked Susan for a real date. Well, I thought it was about time. Will she accept? You'll have to wait and see; the next book is on its way.

Till the next time,
Adrian.

A special thanks

It's all very well having my name on the front cover of this book, but I only had an idea and wrote down a load of words. Thankfully, there are a group of people, who ensure that the story you have just read, is comprehensible and readable; as well as offering me advice on some of the places and situations in the book. This group of people have helped since my first book, I have to admire their fortitude and generosity. I offer my heartfelt thanks, in no particular order, to: Jean, Irene, Claire, Angela, Anthony, Brian and Pete, thank you. Finally, there is the most important person, my wife, who helps me at every stage of the way.

Other books by Adrian Spalding

The Reluctant Detective
The Reluctant Detective Goes South
The Reluctant Detective Under Pressure

Sleeping Malice
Caught on Camera
The Night You Murder

www.adrianspalding.co.uk

Printed in Great Britain
by Amazon